The World of AMAZON PARROTS

DIETER HOPPE

Translated by WILLIAM CHARLTON

The World of Amazon Parrots is a translation, incorporating extensive revisions made by the author, of *Amazonen: Die Arten und Rassen, ihre Haltung und Zucht,* © 1981, 1983 by Eugen Ulmer GmbH & Co., Stuttgart, Germany. English translation © 1992 by T.F.H. Publications, Inc., Ltd. Copyright is also claimed for the illustrations, captions, and such which have been added to this English-language edition.

Photographs: Toni Angermeyer; Dr. Herbert R. Axelrod; Cliff Bickford; Horst Bielfeld; Heiko Bleher; T. Brosset; Tom Caravaglia; Michael DeFreitas; Isabelle Francais; Wolfgang de Grahl; Fred Harris; Dieter Hoppe; Dr. Irwin Huff; Ralph Kaehler; Gary Lilienthal; Courtesy Midori Shobo; Max Mills; A. J. Mobbs; Dr. John Moore; G. Mühlhaus; Dr. E. J. Mulawka; K. T. Nemuras; Stefan Norberg & Anders Hansson; Helmut Pinter; H. Reinhard; Hans Joachim Richter; M. Rosenbaum; Routedale, Ltd.; Linda Rubin; C. Scholtz; Harald Schultz; Vince Serbin; Carol Thiem; Courtesy U.S. Forest Service; Guy van den Bossche; Courtesy Vogelpark Walsrode; Dr. M. M. Vriends.
Drawings: John Quinn; Jürgen Ritter.
Maps: John Quinn.

Title page:
Amazona aestiva, the Blue-fronted Amazon, is a highly regarded member of its genus; its popularity is attributable to its good looks and predictable disposition.

Distributed in the UNITED STATES by T.F.H. Publications, Inc., One T.F.H. Plaza, Neptune City, NJ 07753; in CANADA to the Pet Trade by H & L Pet Supplies Inc., 27 Kingston Crescent, Kitchener, Ontario N2B 2T6; Rolf C. Hagen Ltd., 3225 Sartelon Street, Montreal 382 Quebec; in CANADA to the Book Trade by Macmillan of Canada (A Division of Canada Publishing Corporation), 164 Commander Boulevard, Agincourt, Ontario M1S 3C7; in ENGLAND by T.F.H. Publications, PO Box 15, Waterlooville PO7 6BQ; in AUSTRALIA AND THE SOUTH PACIFIC by T.F.H. (Australia) Pty. Ltd., Box 149, Brookvale 2100 N.S.W., Australia; in NEW ZEALAND by Ross Haines & Son, Ltd., 82 D Elizabeth Knox Place, Panmure, Auckland, New Zealand; in the PHILIPPINES by Bio-Research, 5 Lippay Street, San Lorenzo Village, Makati, Rizal; in SOUTH AFRICA by Multipet Pty. Ltd., P.O. Box 35347, Northway, 4065, South Africa. Published by T.F.H. Publications, Inc. Manufactured in the United States of America by T.F.H. Publications, Inc.

Contents

As the popularity of the amazon parrot grows, so too must the awareness of responsible owners. The betterment of the amazon species relies on caring, inspired treatment of these birds in captivity. This handsome representative is *Amazona ochrocephala oratrix*, the Yellow-crowned Amazon.

Foreword

In only a few months after the appearance of the first German edition of my amazon-parrot book, it was apparent that a large number of bird fanciers and people interested in birds are enthusiastic about this interesting parrot genus, and so it was unavoidable that the German book went out of print in no time at all. As T.F.H. Publications, Inc., has obtained the English-language rights to the book, I have taken this opportunity to revise and in part rewrite the first edition. New findings in systematics as well as breeding successes in captivity were also taken into consideration.

I am very happy about the truly encouraging fact that more and more keepers of amazon parrots are promoting breeding attempts with these birds. One can consider a successful breeding in captivity to be a contribution to the preservation of the species. I wish to make an emphatic appeal to the owners of singly kept cage birds to give up this kind of amazon keeping. Through the purchase of a mate one should foster breeding attempts. Only through future successful breedings in captivity will it be possible to guarantee that amazon parrots will continue to exist.

I wish very sincerely to thank all of the fanciers and breeders who placed their own practical experience and specialized information at my disposal for this book. My special thanks go out to Dr. J. Steinbacher, publisher of the specialty journal *Die Gefiederte Welt*, and to Dr. C. König of the Rosenstein Museum, Stuttgart, who supported me in word and deed. Just as sincerely I wish to thank my correspondents in Europe and North and South America, without whose help the information cited in this book could not have been obtained. I also thank T.F.H. Publications for undertaking the English-language edition.

DIETER HOPPE

Remarkable for its coloration and its ability to mimic is the Saint Vincent's Amazon, *Amazona guildingii*, a rare species whose flight for surivival depends on keeper responsibility and the continued interest in its race.

Life in the Wild

Amazon parrots inhabit the American continents. The border between the United States and Mexico in the north forms the natural limit of their distribution. In the south they range to about 35 degrees south latitude in parts of northern Uruguay and northern Argentina. These parrots are also found on a number of islands of the West Indies. Their range stretches about 9000 kilometers from north to south. In this vast area one finds the most diverse climatic regions and vegetation forms. The 27 species of the genus *Amazona* have adapted to the most varied environments, and thus we find these birds in the riverine regions and forests of the temperate zones as well as in tropical rain forests, deciduous dry forests, savannas, and desert regions. The ranges of the different species vary greatly in size: for example, the Yellow-crowned Amazon, *Amazona ochrocephala*, inhabits an area that stretches from the mouth of the Amazon to the Tres Marias Islands, an archipelago off the western coast of Mexico. In comparison to this range, that of the Yellow-shouldered Amazon, *Amazona barbadensis*, which occurs only in a small coastal area of Venezuela and on the islands of Margarita, Blanquilla, and Bonaire, is very small. "Very small" also characterizes the environments available to the amazon parrots found on the islands of the West Indies. Virtually all of the "Caribal" amazon parrots, with the exception of the Cuban Amazon, *Amazona leucocephala*—which lives on Cuba, the Cayman Islands, and the Bahamas Islands—occur only on one island. The continued existence of these island parrots is, considering the extremely limited space available, much more threatened than that of the mainland amazon parrots.

In the species treatments the distribution of the birds will be considered in more detail. It will be reported, for example, that the range of the Red-necked Amazon, *Amazona arausiaca*, is the island of Dominica in the West Indies. The indicated range only partially reflects the actual

Opposite: The Yellow-crowned Amazon, *Amazona ochrocephala ochrocephala*. *Above:* In their native lands, amazon parrots inhabit riverine and temperate forest regions, as well as deserts, dry forests and rain forests.

conditions, since although the island is relatively small in size, one finds on it the most diverse terrains and climatic and vegetation zones. In the course of its evolution the Red-necked Amazon has become adapted to a particular habitat and can therefore make use of only ten or twenty percent of the available living space. The same applies to the ranges given for the other species.

The social behavior of amazon parrots is often contingent on the environment and the availability of foods—a constant food source deters an individual species's need to wander from area to area. Contentedly feasting is the Blue-fronted Amazon, *Amazona aestiva*.

Although amazon parrots are flocking birds, the social life of an amazon-parrot species is always determined by the environment the birds inhabit. With species or subspecies that live in the tropical rain forest, which exhibits constant climatic and biological conditions, the social behavior of the individual parrots is not as developed as it is among those that inhabit savannas or open woodlands. The amazon parrots that live in the rain-forest zones usually search for food in pairs, and they are very seldom

forced to wander even locally, thanks to the constant supply of food. As a rule, these parrots are permanent residents that spend their lives in a relatively small locality. The amazon parrots that inhabit the tropical forests seldom form large flocks. In the evening hours they assemble at their so-called roosting trees, but seldom does one find flocks of over a hundred birds.

The flocking behavior of amazon parrots that inhabit the zones on the edges of forests, open woodlands, or scrub land is quite different. In these parrots, group behavior is much more pronounced. In their localities one can frequently find many thousands of amazon parrots in the late afternoon hours on their ancestral roosting trees. In the early morning the large congregations split up into small parties in order to search for food. The search for food apparently takes place very systematically. The fruit-bearing trees continue to be visited by the birds until they have been completely harvested. The greater the number of amazon parrots living together in a limited area, the faster they will deplete the available sources of food, so that the birds are forced to wander locally. In contrast to the species that live in tropical forests, the amazon parrots of open regions are so-called partial, or short-distance, migrants, whose home range is determined by the current availability of food. Migratory behavior is very pronounced in the amazon parrot species that are found in the northernmost as well as the southernmost living spaces of the range; that is, Mexico as well as the northern portions of Argentina and the southern parts of Brazil. The Tucuman Amazon (*Amazona pretrei tucumana*), for example, breeds at sites on the eastern slopes of the Andes, then migrates as far as the northeastern Argentine province of Misiones at the end of the breeding season.

The breeding seasons of wild amazon parrots begin in May of each year for the northern species. In the more southern parts of the ranges they are shifted into the previous months; for example, the breeding season begins in February in northern South America. With the amazon parrots living in the southernmost areas, breeding takes place in the period from October to November, the spring months of that region.

The larger amazon parrots become capable of reproduction only in the fifth year, while the smaller species attain sexual maturity after two to three years. With the onset of sexual maturity, the search for a mate begins. It is suspected that the birds mate for life, that they are therefore monogamous. No substantiation of this from observations made in the wild is forthcoming, however. Birds kept in flocks in captivity exhibit such a bonding between males and females, so one assumes that pairing to this extent also occurs in the wild.

At the start of the breeding season

Acting as sentry, the male stays in close vicinity of the nest area during the incubation period. The average clutch size ranges from two to five eggs. This protective pair are White-fronted Amazons, *Amazona albifrons*.

A mating pair of amazons will segregate itself from the flock. Amazons are monogamous parrots that chose partners for life. These two are White-fronted Amazons, *Amazona albifrons*.

the amazon-parrot pairs separate from the flocks and abandon communal behavior until the young have fledged. The contrasting coloration of the tail feathers, bend of the wing, and speculum is particularly significant in courtship. During courtship the wings are positioned in such a way that the colorfully marked areas of plumage are prominently displayed. The male parrots then parade back and forth on the branches and at the same time contract the pupils to the size of a pinhead, so that the typically orangish red color of the iris is especially prominent. The feeding of the female by the male is also part of the courtship ceremonies. Amazon parrots use tree cavities as nesting sites, preferring the higher sites. The chosen breeding sites are stubbornly defended against conspecifics that also show an interest in them. Amazon parrots do not bring in material for lining the

nest. Usually there is only a natural layer of decaying wood on the floor of the nest cavity.

The various species of amazon parrots lay between two and five eggs, which are then incubated only by the female for about 25 to 26 days. During incubation the females leave the nest cavity only for brief periods in order to eat and drink. The males remain in the vicinity of the nests during this time and act as sentries. Since the females begin incubating from the first egg on, the young hatch at the intervals in which the eggs were laid. The little parrots are fed only by the mother bird in the first 8 to 14 days of life. Only when the offspring are somewhat larger does the male participate in feeding them. Whoever has had the good fortune to raise amazon parrots in captivity is aware of the amount of food necessary for rearing the young. In the wild, the parent birds are occupied

When lacking a conspecific, amazons may resolve to mate with parrots of a different species. Hybrid crosses in the amazon-parrot world are met with mixed reception from fanciers. *Amazona amazonica amazonica*, the Orange-winged Amazon, and *A. autumnalis autumnalis*, the Red-lored Amazon.

nonstop from morning till evening in supplying food to the youngsters.

The nestling period of the majority of amazon-parrot species is between 60 and 80 days. After fledging, the young are immediately able to fly and can already fly rather long distances on the first day after leaving the nest. The family unit remains together for many weeks, during which time the young amazons continue to be fed by the parents for a fairly long time.

The ruthless exploitation of nature in the amazon parrots' vast range began with the discovery of the Americas by Columbus. The continually increasing settlement, the unbelievably total deforestation of entire regions, and the growth of farming and industry leave far-reaching, catastrophic wounds that can no longer be healed. The destruction of nature has meanwhile also had a detrimental effect on the continued existence of the amazon parrots; the changes in the environment drive the birds from their homelands. Thus the living space available to them is becoming more and more limited, and it is only a question

of time before the last amazon-parrot species is added to the Red List of endangered species. Amazon parrots, of course, also have natural enemies. They often fall prey to raptors. Rodents, monkeys, snakes, and also other species of birds can cause great damage to nests, eggs, and youngsters.

As tree-cavity nesters, the eggs and young of amazon parrots are especially imperiled by the frequent rains. A short tropical rainfall can, for example, flood the nest cavity and destroy the nest and eggs. Hurricanes, which occur seasonally in September in the islands of the West Indies, are a constant and widespread danger. With their powers of destruction they not only inflict considerable losses on the living population, through the destruction of the available nesting and feeding trees they also damage the amazon parrots' vital necessities for years to come.

For all these reasons, bird fanciers who own an amazon parrot should acquire a mate for it and attempt to breed the birds in captivity, in order to preserve this parrot genus, which is becoming rarer, for future generations.

Amazon Parrots in Captivity

When the first Spaniards reached the West Indies and the American continent, they found tame parrots being kept by the primitive as well as civilized races of Indians. The Indians kept parrots for a very simple reason: the colorful parrot feathers were used for head ornamentation. Additionally, the birds were a living food reserve, like our own chickens. Soon the parrots kept by the Indians found their way to Europe, and at the beginning of the sixteenth century the first South American parrots reached Central Europe as gifts from the Spaniards to the royal courts. In the eighteenth and nineteenth centuries the parrots made their first appearance in the houses of the middle class. At that time the first zoos were also created, in which everyone could admire the still-rare parrots. In this period the bird fancy and an interest in exotic birds also developed, and so amazon parrots too gradually came into the care of bird fanciers. The birds' ability to learn words and complete sentences as well as melodies, and often use them on appropriate occasions, allowed the amazon parrots to be included among the most popular kinds of parrots. In this respect nothing has changed to this day.

Initial Considerations

The keeping of domestic animals by man can be traced as far back as the Stone Age, thanks to historical illustrations and traditions. Thus our relationship with dogs, for example, has already been in place for several millennia.

The appeal of the amazon parrot over other members of the order Psittaciformes has been linked historically to its exquisite plumage as well as its ability to learn phrases and melodies. *Amazona viridigenalis,* the Green-cheeked Amazon.

Yellow-naped
Amazons at eight
weeks of age.
Parrots at this
young age require
a parent's
constant attention
and care.

In our present-day technological world, with its urbanized landscapes, we have a nostalgia for nature. Nowadays many attempt to recreate a bit of nature inside their own four walls. From recent opinion polls one discovers that house plants, from cyclamens to orchids, are tended in virtually every household. Millions of tropical fish move in the tanks of aquarists. From hummingbird to heron, from insect to mammal, virtually every kind of animal is kept by fanciers today. To be sure, there are also many so-called animal lovers who surround themselves with animals out of mistaken idealism or even because of a passion for bragging, but one can certainly find black sheep of this kind anywhere. The purchase of a house pet should always be preceded by a gathering of detailed information and a critical self-examination; only then does one obtain a living creature that demands attention and daily care. A spontaneous purchase on a whim of any kind should certainly be avoided. One must consider beforehand which animal is most appropriate, what demands the singly kept animals make, and what kinds of accommodations are required. One should also consult family members, who will also be affected by the purchase of an animal.

Accommodations

With amazon parrots it is very important to provide accommodations suitable for them. For this reason, one should gather information about suitable cages and determine where in the house the cage will be situated, before the bird is purchased. As nearly as possible, one should choose a bright spot near a window, with the following considerations: A location directly in front of a window is unsuitable, because there is the danger here that a

draft could be produced when the window is opened. Additionally, a location with an extended period of direct sunlight should be avoided. A location next to a heater is also undesirable; the constantly circulating warm air would dry out the animal's plumage and skin and would therefore lead to itching, which in turn could cause the bird to pluck its feathers. The best location for a cage is in a corner of a room, next to a window with sufficient light. It is best to place the cage at eye level. The cage should be as large as possible. A cage floor area of 50 × 50 cm. and a height of about 70 cm. should be the absolute minimum dimensions. A wide selection of parrot cages and indoor flights is offered in the pet shops, so that a satisfactory solution can be found to fit any pocketbook. With a bit of mechanical skill or with the help of someone handy, one can also build the accommodations one's self. When buying or building a cage or flight one should always make sure that a sturdy type of construction, which can stand up to the amazon parrots' bills, is selected. The food bowls in the cage should be installed in such a way that they cannot be soiled or tipped over by the birds. Additionally, the bowls should be readily accessible, so that at the daily feeding time the bowl can also be cleaned. One or more fixtures on which one can fasten fruit or vegetables should also be available. The floor of the cage should be constructed in such a way that it can be removed for cleaning at any time with little effort. At least one natural branch should be available as a perch, which, depending on wear, should be replaced at intervals of two to three weeks. The amazon parrots can satisfy their urge to gnaw on this branch, and, furthermore, they receive trace elements from gnawing the bark and wood.

Only then, when the cage or the

flight has been procured and the exact location in the house has been determined, should the bird be purchased.

Purchasing

As was mentioned in the introduction, the purchase of a living creature should be preceded by a gathering of detailed information. One must be fully aware that the care of a household companion demands a great deal of time. The creature is not just an object that is taken out and put away again on a

Consider the size of the bird, its need for room to stretch its wings, and the number of parrots to be housed when determining the necessary dimensions of the cage. *Amazona aestiva*, the Blue-fronted Amazon, on its perch.

whim. Constant daily attention and care are necessary. Whoever cannot or does not want to sacrifice this time should have enough self-awareness to abandon the thought of keeping pets. Many people have been introduced by accident to the hobby of keeping birds. Sometimes a visit to a zoo or a pet shop awakens the interest, or, while leafing through the daily newspaper, one comes across an advertisement something like the following: "Selling hand-tame, talking amazon parrot." There are many ways in which one can become a bird fancier. In any case, when purchasing an amazon parrot one should pay attention to the following:

(1) Amazon parrots are not bred in captivity in numbers; therefore, there are not so many opportunities to purchase a domestically bred animal.

(2) Observe the available parrots for some time. Notice how the bird reacts when you approach the cage; the bird must not continue to sit apathetically.

The amount of time it takes an amazon parrot to attain adult coloration can be quite variable. An adult Yellow-crowned Amazon, *Amazona ochrocephala ochrocephala*.

Make sure that the bird breathes regularly, that it does not have a nasal discharge, that the eyes are not runny, and that the droppings are not watery.

(3) Young amazon parrots can be recognized by the coloration of the iris. As a rule, the iris of a young amazon parrot is brown. To be sure, the length of time required for the coloration of the iris to change can be extremely variable. With Yellow-crowned Amazons, *Amazona ochrocephala ochrocephala*, reared in Germany, the author was able to make the observation that the iris color of two approximately five-month-old animals differed. In one bird the iris was dark brown and in the other an orangish color was already evident. If the iris color has reached its final stage (refer to the descriptions of the different species), then one should examine the bird's bill and feet. A young amazon parrot has a smooth bill and little scaling on the toes. In older animals, small horny deposits have usually formed on the bill and feet. In some amazon-parrot species and subspecies, the coloration of the plumage can help to determine whether an individual is young or old. For example, the Yellow-headed Amazon, *Amazona ochrocephala oratrix*, is fully colored only after the fifth to seventh year of life. In the young birds of this subspecies, only the front of the head is yellow, and only after several molts does the yellow extend to the nape region.

(4) Make sure that the bird you wish to purchase is currently being offered a suitable diet. The bird should be accustomed to a rich diet with a variety of seeds, nuts, and fruits, since it is very difficult to switch an amazon parrot that eats only sunflower seeds, for example, to a different diet. Moreover, a one-sided diet causes dietary deficiencies and leads to illnesses.

(5) In Germany, every breeder and

importer of parrots is legally required to band the birds and to furnish proof of the banding. The amazon parrot you purchase must be banded. If no leg band is present, then it can be assumed that the bird was illegally imported into Germany or that it came from an unlicensed breeding facility. Do not be surprised if the seller of a parrot asks for your name and signature at the time of the sale. He is legally obligated to do so and must be able to produce a record of the sale at any time. In this way, the location of origin can be traced when an infectious disease appears in a parrot, and only in this way is a systematic counterattack on the disease possible.

(6) The amazon parrot must be transported as expeditiously as possible. When transported over longer distances only shipping boxes that are equipped with a solidly fitted perch should be used. On longer journeys,

food and water must be available to the bird in the shipping container.

Care and Taming
After the purchase, the amazon parrot should be brought to its new home immediately. The water and food bowls should be filled. Other food offerings, such as ears of corn, spray millet, or pieces of apple and a calcium block, should also be put in beforehand, so that they can easily be reached by the amazon parrot at any time. For the first day the bird must be left completely alone. If one considers the long distance the amazon parrot may have covered before reaching its final home, then one will gladly grant this break for rest in the first few days of the period of acclimation, particularly since the bird was subjected to many stressful situations. The parrot must first cope with the climatic changes as well as changes in diet and must try to get

At three months of age, these healthy Yellow-naped Amazons, *Amazona ochrocephala auropalliata*, sit pretty on a natural-branch perch. Be sure that perches are not chemically treated before furnishing them to your parrots.

some rest. Small children, who could frighten the bird with their boisterous movements, should stay away from the cage in the first few days. Other pets that may be present should be allowed in the vicinity of the newcomer only under supervision. Every change or unaccustomed situation can be stressful for the amazon parrot in the initial stage of the acclimation period, and may lead to illness.

One will quickly be able to determine what kinds of food the bird prefers, and with the preferred treats one can attempt gradually to accustom the amazon parrot to the hand. One tries to give the parrot this food with the hand, but in so doing one should always proceed quietly and carefully, avoiding any sudden movements. The bird will not, of course, take the offered food immediately; instead, it

will at first always be concerned with getting away from the threat of the hand. One should persist in offering the food for a few minutes. After a long while the bird will be prepared to take the offered food from the hand. After the amazon parrot has grown used to the new conditions to some degree and eats regularly and well, one may permit the first excursion from the cage. A perch placed on top of the cage, or a climbing tree placed next to it, serves primarily as a "free" perch for the bird. The bird should undertake its first excursion outside of the cage on its own; one merely opens the cage door. In addition, one can place a connecting stick between the cage opening and the free perch to serve as a "bridge" for the excursion. One should never forcibly remove the amazon parrot from its cage if it does not go out on its

"Siegfried," a hand-trained, vocal Yellow-crowned Amazon, *Amazona ochrocephala oratrix.*

Acclimating the parrot to its free perch should be a gradual process. Once the bird is acclimated to its perch, it will remain there for long periods. Preening is a good sign that this Blue-fronted Amazon is comfortable on its perch.

own at first. After a few days the bird will have progressed far enough to be able to find its way out of the cage and back again by itself. Should the amazon parrot happen to leave the free perch, which serves as its place of residence outside the cage, then one should carefully induce it to return again to the perch. Soon it will have learned that the climbing tree is part of its territory, and it will then always return to it after a short flight through the room. It is very important to accustom the bird to its free perch in the first few days; in this way, it will not afterwards fly to cabinets or other pieces of

The ability to talk and the relative boisterousness of parrots vary from species to species. This talkative parrot is *Amazona ochrocephala panamensis*.

furniture when it is not being watched. One should always keep in mind that, with its powerful bill, an amazon parrot can certainly do some damage to furniture and other household objects. When the amazon parrot has become accustomed to its free perch, then it will seldom leave the perch; it is possible that the bird will remain there constantly, and the cage will only be needed as accommodation for the night.

The ability to learn to talk varies considerably in individual amazon parrots. With amazon parrots that live in the wild, it has been observed that they do not learn and mimic strange noises or animal calls. The phenomenon of repeating strange noises could up till now only be demonstrated with animals living in captivity. It appears that the learning of noises, words, and sentences and the whistling of melodies is a kind of

occupational therapy which the animals prescribe for themselves. In the wild, amazon parrots are subject to a set daily routine, so very little time is left to the animals for activities other than the constant search for food and mutual preening. Birds kept singly in captivity, which do not have to search for food, must accustom themselves to an unnatural way of life. They divert themselves out of boredom, which can often lead to behavior not normally exhibited by the species.

In any event, the talent for mimicking is present in amazon parrots and can be enhanced by constantly talking to them. It is recommended to repeat only one word to them continually—names are best. In this connection, the most suitable are two-syllabled words that end in *a* or *o*, for example, *Jako, Riko, Lora, Mama, Papa*. When repeating the words, make sure the same pitch is used as far as possible. Soon the bird will try to mimic the constantly repeated word. It will always take a certain amount of time before the bird repeats it clearly and distinctly. Once the parrot has learned a word and can repeat it reasonably clearly, then it will not be long before new words or noises are added to the repertoire. The author has had the opportunity to see and hear a few amazon parrots that used the learned words in the appropriate situations. One of these amazon parrots said *Good morning* when someone entered the room, and when leaving one heard a *Goodbye*. A different amazon parrot, every time one offered it a treat, said, *Mmm, isn't that nice*, or, if one sprayed it with lukewarm water, *So, another bath*. The various subspecies of the Yellow-crowned Amazon, *Amazona ochrocephala*, and the Blue-fronted Amazon, *Amazona aestiva*, in particular exhibit a great

Peanuts make up an important part of most parrots' menu, though not as vital a component to the diet as sunflower seeds. Engaged in shelling its peanut is a Blue-fronted Amazon.

talent for learning to talk. It must be mentioned, however, that these two amazon parrots, along with the Orange-winged Amazon, *Amazona amazonica*, are the most commonly kept amazon species, and consequently the majority of reports in captivity pertain to these birds.

In the wild, amazon parrots are very fond of being soaked by rain. At the first raindrops they run back and forth on the branches, ruffle their feathers, flap their wings, and hang head down,

It is recommended that captive amazon parrots be kept constantly occupied. After all, amazon parrots are flocking birds that live in the closest possible contact with others of their kind. Captive amazon parrots kept singly therefore turn to a person as a mate in the absence of suitable members of their own species. Constant talking to the bird is essential. As the keeper, one should realize that the bird wastes away both emotionally and physically if one cannot find

Yellow-naped Amazon sticking its neck out. Feeder trays should be placed variously around the cage, within comfortable reach of the bird and never directly beneath the perch.

during which they emit cries of genuine pleasure. Not only for the bird's plumage, but also for their general well-being, is it very important to offer captive amazon parrots a substitute for rain if they are not housed in a flight outdoors. One should spray the birds with lukewarm water from a plant sprayer two or three times a week. If possible, this showering should take place in the morning or afternoon hours, so that the plumage can dry before the birds retire.

enough time for it. Every serious bird fancier and animal lover, if he cannot spend enough time with his bird, should strive to obtain a mate for it.

Feeding and Care

The proper diet is one of the most important prerequisites for healthy amazon parrots. By offering a many-sided, vitamin-rich diet, the bird can develop sufficient resistance so that many illnesses will not even be able to appear. The basic diet for amazon

parrots should be made up of the following seeds: approximately 50% sunflower seeds, striped and white, with the remaining 50% being peanuts, cembra-pine nuts, corn, pumpkin seeds, hulled oats, and possibly raw rice, various kinds of millet, and linseed. Walnuts and Brazil nuts, as well as many other seeds, can be fed as a supplement. Amazon parrots very readily take half-ripe wheat, rye, barley, corn, and so on; one can also offer, depending on the season, fruit and vegetables of all kinds. Apples should not be missing from the daily menu. Cherries, plums, peaches, grapes, apricots, mandarin oranges, and possibly also grapefruits and lemons (without rinds, naturally), figs, mangoes, bananas, lettuce, spinach, cauliflower, Brussels sprouts, carrots, celery, tomatoes, etc., can always be added as supplements to the basic diet. Various kinds of weed seeds, such as dandelion, plantain, shepherd's purse,

among others, as well as haw berries, should be fed seasonally. Amazon parrots are very fond of leaf buds from fruit trees. Of course, when obtaining leaf buds caution must be exercised; one must make sure that one uses twigs from unsprayed trees, since virtually all insecticides are toxic. Sunflower seeds, millets, and other seeds can also be offered in sprouted form. A calcium block should not be missing from any cage or flight. If the parrots only occasionally gnaw on the calcium blocks, then one must purchase edible calcium in powdered form and spread this over the food about twice a week; enough to cover the point of a knife is sufficient. Now and then, one can give the amazon parrots fresh forest soil (for trace elements), and, if possible, sea sand in a dish or similar vessel.

The importance of vitamins and minerals is shown in the following:
VITAMIN A : Critical for growth, maintains vision, affects the various

In its juvenile plumage, this Yellow-crowned Amazon exhibited only a small yellow forehead patch, and was thought to be a Panama Amazon. In time, however, the yellow nape band developed; additionally, the coloration of the bill and toes became darker. This bird should be classified as *Amazona ochrocephala parvipes*.

A vitamin-rich diet increases a young bird's resistance to illness. If this young Blue-fronted Amazon is provided with a suitably varied diet, it will not need additional vitamin supplements at a later age.

skin layers. Vitamin A is found in egg, milk, and cod-liver oil, among others, and as the precursor carotene in carrots, corn, and cruciferous vegetables.

VITAMIN B_1: Regulates carbohydrate metabolism and strengthens the musculature. Vitamin B_1 is contained in yeast, egg yolk, fresh vegetables, and plant seedlings.

VITAMIN B_2: Regulates the conversion of nutriments and promotes growth. Vitamin B_2 is a constituent of, among others, yeast, cod-liver oil, milk, and eggs.

VITAMIN B_6: Essential for blood formation and regulates growth. Vitamin B_6 is a constituent of, among others, grain (if capable of germination) and yeast.

VITAMIN B_{12}: Essential for fat, protein, and carbohydrate metabolism, and accelerates the growth of young birds. Vitamin B_{12} is a constituent of, among others, fish and liver meal, milk, and egg.

VITAMIN C: Strengthens resistance against illnesses, fortifies the tissues, and activates hormones and enzymes. Vitamin C is contained, among others, in fruit, vegetables, and potatoes.

VITAMIN D: Strengthens the skeleton and prevents the laying of thin-shelled eggs. Vitamin D is contained, among others, in cod-liver oil, eggs, and milk.

VITAMIN E: Strengthens sex functioning (only in animals). Vitamin E is contained, among others, in seeds capable of germination or seedlings.

VITAMIN H: Promotes the formation of skin and feathers and nerve cells. Vitamin H is contained, among others, in egg yolk, yeast, and molasses.

VITAMIN K: As the antihemorrhagic vitamin it regulates the coagulating ability of the blood. Vitamin K is contained, among others, in vegetables, stinging nettle, and hemp.

CALCIUM: Essential for strengthening the skeleton and nerves. Contained, among others, in phosphated and carbonated foods and cuttlebone.

IRON: Essential constituent of the red blood corpuscles; contained, among others, in spinach, strawberries, and egg yolk.

IODINE: Promotes functioning of the thyroid gland; contained, among others, in cod-liver oil and garlic.

POTASSIUM: Promotes the growth of the young; contained, among others, in fruit, celery, milk.

COPPER: Prevents anemia and enhances the coloration of the

plumage; contained, among others, in fruit and vegetables.

MANGANESE: Essential for the growth of the young, the skeleton, as well as the plumage; contained, among others, in fruit and leafy vegetables.

MAGNESIUM: Essential for strengthening the bones; contained, among others, in spinach.

PHOSPHORUS: Along with calcium the most important building block for the skeleton; contained, among others, in strawberries.

Every keeper and breeder of parrots should direct his special attention to the composition of the diet. Providing a varied, multifarious diet is the foundation for successfully keeping parrots.

Natural branches should be used as perches for amazon parrots. The birds can satisfy their disposition to gnaw, and, as was previously mentioned, they simultaneously take in trace elements when gnawing the bark and wood. One should make sure that the perches are of different diameters so that the amazon parrots must always grasp with

To clip the wings, scissor the feathers approximately two to three centimeters away from the flesh. With this Double Yellow-head, the primary feathers have been clipped.

their feet in different positions. One should replace them as soon as the bark has been gnawed off or the surfaces have become smooth. If one always offers the amazon parrots perches of different thicknesses, then the normal, natural wearing of the claws is promoted. Only rarely must one trim the claws of amazon parrots that are offered good perches.

As was previously mentioned, amazon parrots enjoy being soaked with rain. Not only for the sake of the plumage, but also for the general well-being of the animal, it is recommended that the birds be sprayed with lukewarm water several times a week. A plant sprayer, which emits a fine mist, is suitable. The shower should always be given in the morning or afternoon hours, and the temperature must not be lower than 18°C. One must make sure that the amazon's plumage does not become thoroughly soaked; the bird must remain able to fly.

If unsuitable perches are used, the claws may not be worn sufficiently and can become too long. One can trim the claws with a sharp knife or sturdy scissors. When cutting the claws the utmost caution is necessary; under no circumstances should one cut into the quick, since there is a danger that the claw could become deformed or that the toe could become infected.

One must be just as careful when trimming the upper mandible as when trimming the claws. Normally the tip of the upper mandible is worn away on its own—assuming that branches or pieces of wood for gnawing are available to the amazon parrot—so that the tip of the bill will rarely grow so long that it requires trimming. Under no circumstances should the living portion be injured when cutting. Inexperienced keepers should first consult an expert (for example, an animal dealer or a veterinarian) or leave the trimming to the expert.

Amazon parrots will fly in small rooms or flights only with great reluctance; they prefer to cover the distance by climbing. Amazon parrots are very fond of spending the summer in an outdoor flight in the garden or on a balcony. Building an outdoor flight will not be possible everywhere; if one still wishes to put one's amazon parrot out in the fresh air, then one should first clip the bird's flight feathers. The amazon parrot must not be put on a chain, since the danger of injury is too great; and besides, if the chain gets tangled, then the bird's range of movement will be limited considerably. To clip the flight feathers one must take the bird in the hand and then spread the wings. With the aid of scissors one cuts the secondaries and primaries about two to three centimeters away from the flesh. The two outermost primaries should not be clipped, since only then will the wings retain a presentable appearance when they are folded.

Time after time we find that parrots pluck out or chew off their own feathers. Cockatoos (*Cacatua*), macaws (*Ara*), and Grey Parrots (*Psittacus*) especially display a marked tendency toward feather plucking. Amazon parrots rarely exhibit this vice. It is very difficult to cure a parrot that pulls out or bites off its own feathers. The plucking can take on extreme forms. The author frequently saw completely bare birds that were only feathered on the head and neck. What causes this abnormal plucking has not yet been thoroughly explained. Apparently there are several contributory factors. Vitamin and mineral deficiencies would seem to be a fundamental cause. Boredom, overly dry room air, salt deficiency, unsuitable accommodations, psychoses, and other conditions also appear to lead to feather plucking. A successful treatment for curing the usually psychologically disturbed parrots does not exist. It is striking that, for the most part, it is parrots kept alone purely as house pets that "mutilate" themselves by feather plucking. Parrots kept in flocks or in pairs seldom acquire this vice. In the

meantime, medications, sprays, and various kinds of foods were developed for the so-called feather pluckers, but unfortunately the remedies marketed by the industry produce few cures. In any case, it is better to place the singly kept bird with a mate, or one should decide to give the feather plucker to a fancier who keeps a number of birds— if possible, of the same species. Feather plucking seldom can be cured in any other way, at least not permanently.

Illness

Even though amazon parrots may be housed in cages and aviaries, they are still exposed to dangers that can lead to disease or injury. In animal keeping of any kind, cleanliness should be the ruling precept, since adherence to a hygienic routine will do more than anything else to avert illness. However, injury and disease cannot be avoided

Typically, amazons in a small flight cage will merely climb about; only with great reluctance will they fly. For breeding purposes, however, cages like this one may be what's needed.

A Yellow-crowned Amazon wears an Elizabethan collar, a standard device placed around the bird's neck to prevent it from plucking itself.

totally, and the care of hurt or sick animals is the province of the veterinarian. The symptoms of illness are often the result of the most diverse causes, so that a correct diagnosis is possible only after a thorough investigation. A veterinarian should be consulted at the first appearance of an illness, for example, when a bird begins to sit around with fluffed feathers or to breathe abnormally or when behavior that is not normal is observed. One should not stand by and wait, hoping that the bird will get well by itself, without treatment. An illness can be cured much more quickly in its early stages, while the bird is still in good condition and can receive the prescribed medication without difficulty.

A detailed description of the signs of the various avian diseases is beyond the scope of this book; therefore, the following section considers only the diseases that may be life-threatening to the birds and under certain conditions can also present a danger to people.

PSITTACOSIS/ORNITHOSIS. Parrot fever (psittacosis) is a viral infection that can take on epizootic forms and can also cause illness in humans. In 1874, it was noted that contact with diseased parrots transmitted the disease to people. Many individuals who contracted the disease died. In 1934 [in Germany], the so-called Psittacosis Law was put into effect, and at the same time all infected parrot stocks were depopulated. Following the development by the pharmaceutical industry of effective medicines and in view of the number of successful cures that could be achieved, a law was promulgated by the cabinet minister for Food, Agriculture, and Forests on October 1, 1970: the Ordinance for Protection against Psittacosis and Ornithosis (Psittacosis Ordinance).

In spite of the intensive tetracycline treatment of parrots newly imported into Germany, 200 to 300 cases of human infection are reported annually. Every outbreak, or even the suspicion of the presence psittacosis, must be reported to the proper authority, as well as to the official veterinarian. As a breeder and keeper of parrots, it is one's obligation to have his stock of birds examined for psittacosis at least once a year, as a preventive measure. All state laboratories conduct such tests from freshly collected stool specimens. Because psittacosis is contagious and widespread, it is recommended that newly acquired parrots always be segregated and acclimated in separate accommodations. At the same time, freshly collected stool specimens should be delivered to the laboratory for testing. Newly acquired birds should be put together with other birds only when it is a hundred percent certain that the new arrival is healthy. Always keep in mind that the introduction of psittacosis organisms can cause the entire stock of healthy birds to become sick or to die, within a very short time. In addition, always keep in mind that the virus presents a serious and perhaps even deadly threat to people.

The clinical picture of psittacosis in the parrot shows very unspecific signs, which in the early stages can often lead to a false diagnosis. Often one can recognize the illness by a viscous nasal discharge, lack of appetite, and labored and heavy breathing. Furthermore, the diseased birds appear apathetic, sleep constantly, and are fluffed up when they perch. Such signs, however, also appear in other diseases. Therefore, in order to be assured of an unequivocal diagnosis, one should immediately collect fresh stool specimens from the sick animal and send them to a state laboratory. Should the results of the tests confirm the presence of psittacosis, treatment must commence

immediately. In addition, the directives of the veterinary officials must be followed.

Good cures can be achieved with a soft food containing chlortetracycline, providing a fresh mixture daily. With the smaller parrots and parakeets, the preparation is given for thirty days; larger parakeets and parrots receive it for forty-five days. Amazon parrots that have acute psittacosis and refuse nourishment must first be treated by injection. A one-time injection of 300 mg. of an oil-based solution of Chloromycetin (chloramphenicol) or similar antibiotic will be sufficient in most cases. Following this, most birds will eat again. To obtain a cure, one continues the medicated food. Effective treatment will produce a blood level of 1.0 mcg./ml. from a blood sample taken on the tenth day of treatment.

SALMONELLOSIS (PARATYPHOID). Salmonella infections can occur in animals and people. These microorganisms are always communicable, even to birds. The bacteria, of which 1600 different

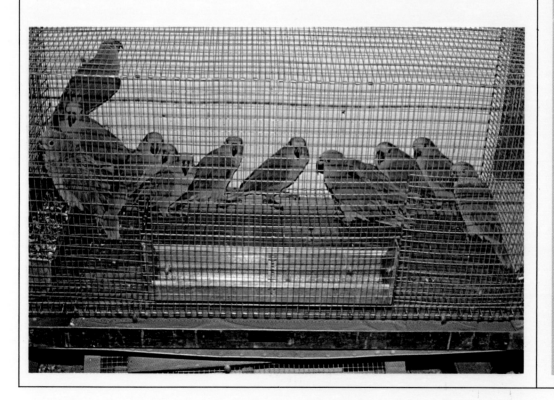

The conditions of transport most often lend themselves to overcrowding, thus the necessity of quarantine is eminent.

In general, transmission of disease between pet amazons and people is uncommon, but it can occur. Consultation with a physician or a veterinarian offers the best chance of averting such illnesses.

species are known, can be shed by so-called carriers, people or animals who outwardly appear completely healthy, at irregular time intervals. These disease carriers constitute the greatest source of danger to a healthy bird. In addition, the danger of salmonellosis always exists, even when amazons are kept singly. Infected people, utensils, cages, etc., constantly present a risk. The clinical picture of salmonellosis is quite varied; only through laboratory testing can the disease be unequivocally diagnosed. In the acute intestinal form of salmonellosis, the diseased animals will perch listlessly and suffer from diarrhea with extremely loose droppings. The cerebral form produces disturbances of the nervous system, and victims are frequently afflicted with lameness and cramps. The so-called arthritic form, a chronic form of the disease, is recognizable by wing or leg crippling. In the case of live animals, as was mentioned, certain diagnosis is possible only through laboratory examination of the droppings, from which the bacteria may be isolated.

Following diagnosis, antibiotic treatment which will lead to the recovery of the ill birds should be initiated. The initial dose of the medicine should be injected, as this is the quickest way to achieve a proper level of the medicine in the tissues. Further treatment should be undertaken via the food or drinking water. Birds suffering from salmonellosis should generally be housed in a separate location. All objects in the vicinity of the cage should be disinfected every other day until the conclusion of the treatment. Fourteen days after the end of treatment, a test of the droppings must again be done in the laboratory in order to confirm the success of the treatment.

NEWCASTLE DISEASE (FOWL PEST). In recent years there have been repeated outbreaks of fowl pest. It was observed not only in poultry but also in other birds, including parrots. This viral infection can run a devastating course and do a tremendous amount of damage to a stock of birds in a very short time. Four or five days after infection, the ill birds manifest a loss of appetite and a rise in body temperature. They hide in darkened corners and exhibit watery diarrhea, labored breathing, and fluffed feathers. Neurological reactions may also be observed: rotating the head 180 degrees, lameness, and cramps (Dr. Aeckerlein). The signs and the course of the disease can vary greatly, so it is difficult to recognize it. Transmission to other birds can occur through air, utensils, or dust. Certain diagnosis is possible only from a dead animal, through evidence of the virus or a hemagglutination-inhibition test. As with all viral infections, no treatment seems to be possible. It is known, however, that the disease organism shows less resistance when exposed to strong ultraviolet radiation. Therefore, it is recommended as a preventive and as supportive treatment that the birds be housed in bright daylight and, possibly, that supplementary ultraviolet lighting be provided. Extra doses of vitamins can also strengthen the bird's own defenses. A law requiring the inoculation of new imports with a vaccine while they are in the quarantine station has been under consideration, because only a systematic preventive campaign of this kind can effectively limit the further incidence and spread of the disease.

WORMS. In larger breeding installations there is always the danger of diseases involving worms. It is well known that birds in the wild are often subject to various worm parasites. An attack of worms in aviary birds can have the most severe consequences and, under certain circumstances, can result in the loss of the entire stock of birds. The incidence and spread of parasitic worms is always a possibility. A parasite-free stock can become completely infested by worms by the introduction of only one bird that is carrying them. For example, a female roundworm produces several thousand eggs per day, which the bird then excretes. With favorable temperatures and sufficient moisture, conditions which are always present in an aviary, the eggs develop into viable larvae. Birds foraging and feeding on the aviary floor may ingest the worm larvae. To keep one's birds permanently free of worms, one must observe at least the minimal hygienic requirements when constructing the aviary and in keeping the premises and its accessories clean. Roundworms (ascarids) and threadworms (*Capillaria* spp.) are widespread and can often cause the death of an afflicted bird.

In most cases, there is no special clinical picture for a bird with a worm infestation; without regular examination of the birds' droppings, diagnosis is impossible. Depending on the kind of parasite, specific medicines are available to treat worm infestations (e.g., Dekelmin or Eustidil). The correct dosage can be obtained by consulting the instructions

Owners should observe their birds for signs of ill health. The plumage of the Blue-front shown preening here is in fine condition.

accompanying the medicine. A follow-up of the same preparation may be given four weeks after the initial treatment. With a small stock of birds, the medicine should be given directly: by means of an eyedropper or injected into the breast muscles.

Concomitant with the medication, the aviary itself and all utensils must be disinfected. Earth floors must be turned over to a depth of about 20 cm. Trellises, food and water dishes, perches, and other aviary equipment should be treated with a disinfecting agent (Dekaseptol, for example). Possibly the nonflammable parts of the aviary can be heated briefly with a propane torch. As already mentioned, with constantly changing stock, or with parrots kept in outdoor flights, droppings should be examined regularly. Newly acquired birds should generally be kept in acclimation cages. Only after one is sure that they are healthy and wormfree can they be transferred to aviaries with other birds.

The Hawk-headed Parrot, *Deroptyus accipitrinus,* is a species closely allied to the amazon parrots.

Breeding

The great population explosion and the continual expansion of industrial and agricultural areas on the Latin American continent are displacing amazon parrots from their primal homelands. The natural environment available to the birds is becoming more and more limited, and so it is inevitable

females. As a rule, male birds have a proportionately larger head and bill. To be sure, this character is not dependable a hundred percent of the time, especially since the side-by-side comparison of several individuals is required. Certainty in sexing can be had from an endoscopic examination. Firms that import parrots, those that own quarantine stations and employ veterinarians, will perform these examinations at the buyer's request.

Pairing together two well-suited parrots is an oftimes difficult task. One can assume that this pair of Red-lored Amazons is quickly striking up a promising relationship.

that the survival of the different species and subspecies of amazons is already imperiled. The ruthless exploitation of nature appears to be unavoidable and unstoppable. As serious bird fanciers, we should therefore at least feel obligated to preserve the amazon forms held in captivity for future generations by attempting to breed them.

In the majority of amazon-parrot species it is very difficult to distinguish the sexes, since no reference points of any kind, such as plumage coloration or body size, differentiate males from

The sexing procedure amounts to a minor out-patient operation, with no permanent damage of any kind.

Amazon parrots are thought to be monogamous throughout their lives, even though they form flocks with members of their own species or with related species outside of the breeding season. This means that the birds in the wild do not choose their mates indiscriminately. This is a natural ingrained behavior that increases the breeder's difficulty in putting together a compatible pair for breeding. The

optimal arrangement for pairing entails placing about eight to ten animals of the same species together in a large flight. After a certain amount of time spent becoming accustomed to one another, pairs will separate from the flock of their own accord. If one is certain that he has a true pair, it is advisable to mark the birds with leg bands; for example, males red and females blue, or some kind of band that can be differentiated just as easily. If one happens to own several pairs of the same species, then it is advisable to additionally mark the pairs that belong together. This has the advantage that one can house the animals in a flock outside of the breeding season.

Some amazon-parrot fanciers have turned to keeping their animals in a flock the year round, during the breeding season as well. Of course, this practice requires very large flights with sufficient space for the individual birds, a sufficient number of nest boxes—at least as many nest boxes as amazon-parrot pairs—and, as far as possible, introducing all of the birds to the flight at the same time. The birds must, of course, be closely observed when they are first placed together, so that one can immediately remove any that prove to be biters. For instance, Fink housed his Hispaniolan Amazons in this fashion, and the breeding success so far—16 youngsters— demonstrates the value of keeping amazon parrots in flocks. The small Caribal amazon parrots, notably the subspecies of the White-fronted Amazon, *Amazona albifrons*, seem especially suited to this method of keeping. With the other species of amazon parrots, extreme caution is necessary during the courtship and breeding seasons if they are kept in flocks. The author attempted on several occasions to keep in-season parrots in a flock; his experiences made the dangers of doing so very clear.

Spacious outdoor flights with attached shelter rooms are ideal for successful breeding. The space in which the parrots will be housed for breeding should be as large as possible. When building a flight, the width should not be less than about 1 m. The flight's length should not be less than 2.50 m., and the shelter room adjoining the outdoor flight should have a floor area of about one m². There is ample specialty literature on building and furnishing aviaries, which makes it superfluous to treat the subject in greater detail here. It should not go unsaid, however, that in designing an aviary for amazon parrots one should make sure the wire partitions that divide the space into flights are installed in such a way that they can be removed with little manipulation. By removing the partitions when the breeding season is over, one can offer one's charges ideal accommodations, since they then have the opportunity to associate as a flock.

Virtually all species of parrots are cavity nesters. In the wild, the animals primarily use abandoned woodpecker holes. If nest sites are scarce, then birds ready to breed will accept alternatives. Thus, amazon-parrot nests have been found in crevices in walls and cliffs, in termitaria, and in holes in river banks. For amazons in captivity, hollowed-out tree trunks are the best nest sites. The cavity of the tree trunk should be 30 cm. wide and about 50 cm. deep. The entrance hole must be located in the upper third of the cavity. The diameter of the entrance hole should vary in size depending on the species of amazon, being 9–15 cm. Supports should be placed inside the breeding cavity to allow the birds to climb down to the floor easily; gouged furrows are thought to be best for this purpose. Using pegs or wire mesh is discouraged because there is too great a danger of injury with these materials,

particularly to youngsters. It is advantageous if one can install several nest boxes, so that the parrots themselves can choose the one they prefer. Amazon parrots use nest boxes only during the courtship, nesting, and nestling periods; the nests are not used for sleeping. Therefore, it is advisable to remove the nest boxes at the end of the breeding season. After they are taken out of the flight, they must be cleaned and disinfected, so they will be ready again at the start of the next breeding season.

In their Latin American homelands, the breeding seasons of amazon parrots begin between October and May. This breeding period will be retained if the animals are kept under ideal conditions in captivity. This means that the amazon parrots living in southern South America begin with courtship in October; those living in northern South America begin in January or February, and the birds occurring in northern Mexico begin in April or May. It is

Opposite: **Amazons are monagamous in their breeding fashion—pairs will remain together for life. Since propagation is so utterly vital to the continued survival of the amazon in captivity, breeding pairs should never be separated.** *Below:* **Sharing a perch are** *Amazona aestiva* **and** *A. ochrocephala oratrix.*

Understanding the details of a parrot species's life in the wild is crucial for creating the proper breeding environment for a given pair. These handsome birds are Lilac-crowned Amazons.

Opposite: New birds should be kept singly before introducing them to other aviary members. *Amazona ochrocephala ochrocephala*, the Yellow-crowned Amazon.

important that the breeder know at which time the parrots in his care will come into breeding condition. For this reason, gathering of information about the life in the wild for the pertinent amazon-parrot species is a basic requirement for any attempt at breeding them. One should also inform himself about the habitats and climatic zones natural to his parrots. Amazon parrots that in the wild live in tropical rain forests must be accommodated differently from animals that inhabit dry, temperate climatic zones, if breeding is to be successful in captivity. The humidity, an important factor in successful breeding, must be controllable so that optimal, natural conditions are present for the amazon-parrot species in question. A hygrometer, with which the existing humidity can be measured at any time, should be found in every aviary, just as a thermometer is.

The fact that amazon parrots do not become sexually mature until they are between two and six years old makes successful breeding even more difficult. This means that if a breeder obtains young amazons, then he must invest much time and patience before sexually mature animals have formed compatible pairs. It is also difficult, if one already has several amazon parrots, to integrate newly purchased birds. In this case one must proceed with extreme caution and follow certain rules. Newly acquired birds belong in an acclimation cage or flight, and only when it is certain that they are healthy should they be brought into contact with the established birds. It is not recommended, however, that the new birds be housed with the others; on the contrary, they should be kept in a nearby flight at first. If no such enclosure is available, then a wire-mesh partition must be installed in the flight to make a section for the new birds separate from the older ones. The new

Captive-bred birds are easier to handle than those which have been removed from the wild. The acquaintance procedure in any case need not be rushed. *Amazona aestiva*.

birds can then gradually become accustomed to the accommodations without being oppressed by others of their own kind. Only at the point in time when the new parrot has become used to its new environment, no longer reacts with panic, and has also learned to recognize the established birds through visual contact, is it possible to allow direct contact between the birds by removing the partition. One should never put together parrots that are not acquainted with one another, since the new birds cannot withstand the attacks of others of their own kind and will continue also get the worst of it in the future. The author once observed how a newly acquired Blue-fronted Amazon, *Amazona aestiva*, was for reasons of space put into a flight occupied by a pair of Rose-ringed Parakeets, *Psittacula krameri*. The two parakeets attacked the much larger Blue-fronted Amazon, which did not take any defensive measures but instead attempted to escape from the danger zone by fleeing. Even as time passed, the parakeets proved to be more than a match for the amazon parrot; although the amazon settled down well in the flight, it always stayed a respectful distance from the parakeets.

If one is in the fortunate position of owning a sexually mature, compatible pair of amazon parrots, then one can observe how the birds court each other at the start of the breeding season. With spread, drooping wings, spread tail feathers, and extremely contracted pupils, the males strut around the females. This spectacle usually takes place in the morning and evening hours; toward its conclusion and before copulation, the feeding of the hen by the cock takes place. The hens first show an interest in the available nest boxes at the beginning of the courtship period. After a suitable nest box has been found, the female examines the nest cavity as closely as possible. The female then frequently disappears inside the box for fairly long periods of time, in order to carry out the final embellishment activities through intensive gnawing. Wood shavings, or layers of soil or humus placed in the nest boxes, are in most cases removed by the birds. During the courtship period, which lasts about 14 days, they behave very noisily, whereby, under certain circumstances, they often emit deafening screeches for hours on end. From this point on, the birds become ill-tempered toward related species as well as the keeper. That is to say they defend their territory instinctively, particularly the area around the nest cavity. This behavior can intensify to such a degree that they attack the keeper as soon as he enters the aviary.

This defensive behavior is even more pronounced in the female than in the male. It is advisable to limit aviary cleaning to only the most necessary activities during the breeding season, so as to disturb the birds as little as possible during the courtship, incubation, and nestling periods.

The female lays the first egg in the nest cavity about 10–14 days after the start of courtship and starts to incubate immediately. Additional eggs are laid at intervals of two days. A clutch can consist of up to five eggs. Amazon-parrot hens must be closely observed during the egg-laying period, so that if egg binding should occur, one can immediately intervene and take action, such as lower-body massage. In serious cases a veterinarian should be consulted without delay. Nest boxes that can be inspected from the outside are very convenient to monitor the hen's condition. After the eggs are laid, nest boxes should only be inspected when the hen is not in the box. The female alone incubates the eggs. During this time, the males stay in the vicinity of the entrance hole, guarding the nest site. The females leave the nest cavity for a short time in the morning and the evening to defecate, feed, and drink. The incubation period is about 25–26 days in all amazon-parrot species. Thereafter, the young hatch in the order in which the eggs were laid. The young amazons produce a faint peeping already on the first day of life. The totally naked, blind hatchlings are fed only by the female in the first

A promising pair of Tucuman Amazons, *Amazona pretrei tucumana*. The courting ritual in parrots is always a delight to witness, one of the many advantages to owning and keeping a breeding pair of parrots.

weeks of life. The male will participate in direct feeding at a later point in time. The youngsters' eyes open at the age of about two weeks; simultaneously, the first feather sheaths push through the skin. Feathering of the young now makes rapid progress, and soon the first green feathers can also be discerned. Considering the unbelievable appetite that is concomitant with the amazon parrots' growth, large amounts of food should be provided. Curds, egg, vegetables, and fruit should be provided as rearing food, in addition to the usual seeds. In such cases, the author offers baby food manufactured by Nestle and Alete, which are available in powder form and can be stirred with warm water into a thick pap. The youngsters leave the nest cavity, completely feathered and almost as large as the adults, between the sixtieth and eightieth day of life. At this point they are completely capable of flight, but their movements are still somewhat awkward; a few days later, however, they are able to move as well as the parents. A short time after leaving the nest the young try to take food themselves, but they continue to be fed by the adults for an extended time. The parents seldom come into breeding condition again after rearing is completed. For this reason, it is advisable to leave the youngster with the parents; there is no reason to separate them unless quarreling takes place.

Occasionally, for no apparent reason, the adults abandon their offspring and take no further notice of the begging calls. One must then assume the task of rearing the young. One removes the youngsters from the nest box and places them in a large carton which has been lined with several layers of paper. The young must be fed at intervals of four to six hours. For this purpose one uses a syringe. A rubber bicycle-tire valve stem is pushed onto the spout and fastened so that it cannot come loose. The syringe is filled with a vitamin-rich, slightly thick pap, preferably baby food, at a temperature

Observe the continually growing plumage on this six-week-old Yellow-naped Amazon, *Amazona ochrocephala auropalliata*.

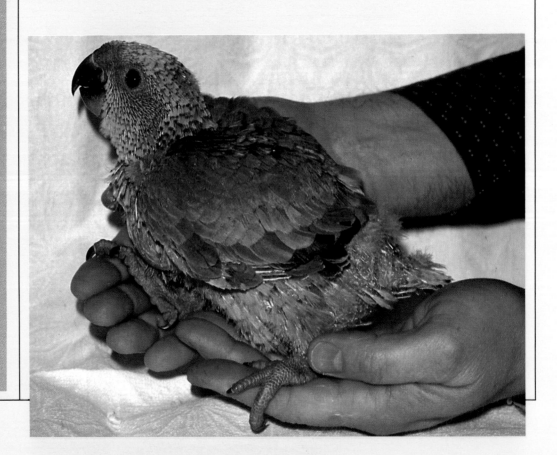

of about 35°C. One inserts the rubber tip in the youngster's bill and then carefully squeezes the food into the little parrot's gullet. Later, when the chicks are somewhat bigger, the pap can be given with a teaspoon, the sides of which are bent upward. Spilled food that may remain on the bill or the plumage must be removed immediately; otherwise the youngster's plumage will become matted. That birds reared by hand become especially tame goes without saying.

As a breeder of parrots, one is obligated to take note of certain legal regulations. These will be considered briefly in the next section.

Breeding Permits
[In Germany,] every fancier is obligated, if he plans to breed birds of the order Psittaciformes, to apply for an authorization permit from the appropriate governmental agency. According to the regulation for protection against psittacosis and ornithosis (Psittacose-Verordnung: Bundesgesetzblatt, Jahrgang 1975, Teil 1), every breeder is obligated to keep an official breeding register and to save it for at least two years after the last entry.

The following entries should be made: (1) Species of animal. (2) Band number and the date of banding. (3) Date of acquisition or other entry into the stock, as well as the animal's provenance. (4) Date of sale and the recipient of the animal, or date of animal's death. (5) Initiation, duration, and results of treatment against psittacosis, as well as the kind of medicine and dosage used.

Additionally, during an outbreak of

Orange-winged and Blue-fronted Amazons. If amazons of different species are housed together, they may form a pair bond and attempt to breed. In view of the status of the amazon parrots generally, it is preferable that they pair with conspecifics.

an infectious disease, every keeper and breeder of amazon parrots is obligated to immediately notify the government veterinarian and the appropriate authorities and then comply with their instructions.

The Washington Convention (CITES)

On March 3, 1973, a treaty was signed in Washington to regulate the international trade in endangered species of wild fauna and flora. The purpose of the treaty is to regulate the

Parrots instinctively recognize the value of gnawing on their perches, thus natural-wood branches are recommended for use with amazons.

trade in species of fauna and flora which are in danger of extinction and simultaneously to guarantee that species threatened with imminent extinction may no longer be used for commercial purposes. The Bundestag of the Federal Republic of Germany, with ratification by the Bundesrat, passed the law to become a signatory to the Washington Convention on May 2, 1975. The promulgation of the law appeared on May 28, 1975, in the Bundesgesetzblatt, Nr. 35, Seite 773–883.

The nations party to the Washington Convention have compiled the following communiqué as a preamble to the regulations:

RECOGNIZING that the fauna and flora living in the wild constitute in their beauty and complexity an irreplaceable component of the natural system of the earth, it behooves us to protect them for present and future generations;
ACKNOWLEDGING that the significance of wild fauna and flora constantly increases in esthetic, scientific, and cultural terms, and in respect to health and the economy as well;
RECOGNIZING that peoples and nations can protect their wild fauna and flora best, and that they should protect them;
RECOGNIZING that the international cooperative effort for the protection of designated species of wild fauna and flora from excessive exploitation by international trade is vitally important;
ACKNOWLEDGING the necessity

to take appropriate measures without delay . . .

Articles I to XXV of the treaty provide definitions of categories. In Appendices I to III, species which face extinction, species which are threatened, and species worth protecting are enumerated. In Appendix I of the Washington Convention, the species especially in danger of extinction are listed. In order to guarantee the survival of these species, which in many instances already seems extremely doubtful, traffic in these specimens is illegal. Only in exceptional cases can the appropriate scientific official grant a special permit; but special permits can never be granted for purposes of

A boisterous Blue-fronted Amazon voices its concerned opinion of the CITES treaty.

Not all parrots are as fortunate as this charming devil, *Amazona ochrocephala auropalliata*, the Yellow-naped Amazon, a race which does not suffer the threat of extinction as do many of its amazon brethren.

commercial trade.

It is interesting to the macaw fancier to note that the Glaucous Macaw (*Anodorhynchus glaucus*), Lear's Macaw (*Anodorhynchus leari*), and Spix's Macaw (*Cyanopsitta spixii*) are listed in Appendix I of the Washington Convention.

The following species and subspecies of genus *Amazona* are listed in Appendix I of the Washington Convention:

Amazona arausiaca (Red-necked Amazon)
A. barbadensis (Yellow-shouldered Amazon), all subspecies
A. brasiliensis (Red-tailed Amazon)
A. guildingii (St. Vincent Amazon)
A. imperialis (Imperial Amazon)
A. leucocephala (Cuban Amazon), all subspecies
A. pretrei pretrei (Red-spectacled Amazon)
A. rhodocorytha (Red-crowned Amazon)
A. versicolor (St. Lucia Amazon)
A. vinacea (Vinaceous Amazon)
A. vittata vittata (Puerto Rican Amazon)

Additional Central and South American parrots from Appendix I are:

Pyrrhura cruentata (Blue-throated Conure)
Rhynchopsitta pachyrhyncha (Thick-billed Parrot), all subspecies
Aratinga guarouba (Golden Conure)
Pionopsitta pileata (Pileated Parrot)

Of the Old World parrots from the African, Asian, and the Australasian-Oceanic regions, the following birds are listed in Appendix I:

Psittacus erithacus princeps (Grey Parrot)
Psittacula echo (Mauritius Parakeet)
Strigops habroptilus (Kakapo)
Cyanoramphus auriceps forbesi (Yellow-fronted Parakeet)
Cyanoramphus novaezelandiae (Red-fronted Parakeet), all subspecies
Geopsittacus occidentalis (Night Parrot)
Neophema chrysogaster (Orange-bellied Grass-Parakeet)
Neophema splendida (Scarlet-chested Grass-Parakeet)
Opopsitta (*Cyclopsitta*) *diophthalma coxeni* (Double-eyed Fig-Parrot)
Psephotus chrysopterygius (Golden-shouldered Parrot), all subspecies
Psephotus pulcherrimus (Paradise Parakeet)

The species listed in Appendix II of the Washington Convention can be marketed only under the condition that in every case the government-designated authority of the exporting country has issued an export permit. An export permit can be issued only if the following conditions are met: (a) If the scientific authority of the exporting country has announced that this exportation is not detrimental to the survival of the species. (b) If the executive authority of the exporting country has confirmed that the specimen has not been obtained through violation of the legal prescriptions promulgated by the country for the protection of animals and plants. (c) If the executive authority of the exporting country has confirmed that every live specimen will

additions were made to Appendices I and II, and the Federal Republic of Germany reported no reservations. Since June 6, 1981, these amendments have been in effect in their entirety for the Federal Republic of Germany. In New Delhi it was decided, among other things, to add to Appendix I three additional amazon-parrot species (*Amazona arausiaca*, *A. barbadensis*, and *A. brasiliensis*), Coxen's Double-eyed Fig-Parrot (*Cyclopsitta*

The Blue-fronted Amazon in profile.

be prepared for transport and dispatched so that the danger of injury, damage to health, and animal suffering will be eliminated as much as possible.

Importation into the Federal Republic of Germany is thus only possible when the exporting country fulfills the above-mentioned conditions (a) through (c).

After the third conference of the signatories to the Washington Convention (which met February 25–March 8, 1981, in New Delhi)

diophthalma coxeni), and both subspecies of the Thick-billed Parrot (*Rhynchopsitta pachyrhyncha*). (These birds have already been included in the lists above.) It was further agreed to place all the parrot species, except those already mentioned in Appendix I, on Appendix II of the Washington Convention. The only exceptions are the Cockatiel (*Nymphicus hollandicus*), the Rose-ringed Parakeet (*Psittacula krameri*), and the Budgerigar (*Melopsittacus undulatus*). To these three

The preservation of the birds in captivity as well as the birds' native habitats remain the focus of wild-life activists. The beauty and personality of this Yellow-crowned Amazon hopefully will inspire more support for these worthy causes.

species, Appendix III of the Washington Convention applies.

This new resolution binds the treaty nations to supervision of a hundred percent of the parrot trade. Should the scientific authorities of the exporting nations confirm that commerce involving one species or another becomes harmful to the species, they can suspend trade at any time.

The regulation of commerce in parrots by Appendices I and II of the Washington Convention is a welcome precaution; however, the menace of habitat destruction, the root of the entire problem, is not addressed. In the opinion of the author, the threat to avian species originates first and foremost with the destruction and exploitation of the natural environment. Day after day, mankind sacrifices vast biotopes and thereby destroys the biocoenosis, the living community of animals and plants. Even now, very few parrot species of parrots are in a position to adjust to the environmental changes wrought by

man. With good reason, one must ask the question: Why are animals and plants, with no chance of survival in the wild, not placed in the hands of experts (fanciers or scientific institutions)?

The following instance of species decline seen from the point of view of the parrot fancier is presented for governmental authorities to take into consideration in their future decision making.

The wild population of the Puerto Rican Amazon, *Amazona vittata*, was estimated in 1968 to be 15–20 birds. An assistance program with a permanent staff was formed for the preservation of the species, even though from a genetic point of view it seems questionable whether survival is possible at all. A program was developed under the best possible conditions in Luquillo National Forest Reserve, the last refuge of the Puerto Rican Amazon. So far, the success achieved has been small: the stock has been kept almost constant. Apparently the assistance program will be ended, since it was recognized that changes in habitat conditions do not offer the amazon parrots any chance of survival. In a few years, the Puerto Rican Amazons will be completely gone. In this case it is easy to understand how changes in the natural environment brought about by mankind can be responsible for the extinction of one animal species; it will be the same with other parrot species. Why don't we consider putting the last wild Puerto Rican parrots into the care of experienced parrot breeders? There are certainly many breeders or associations of breeders which would be in a position, through appropriate accommodations and care suitable to the species, to preserve the birds for future generations through successful breeding. The birds could be sheltered from all natural and environmental factors, so one assumes that the population will recover. Subsequent reintroduction would certainly be possible.

Lovers of nature and animals must look on with sadness and disillusionment as more and more ecosystems, the foundations of our lives, which took millennia to develop, are being sacrificed within a very short time for so-called progress. What is the sense of laws, such as the Washington Convention for the protection of species, which regulate the commerce in threatened species but fail to prevent the destruction of their native environment?

In any case, parrot owners and breeders must in the future note the following points: With the intended purchase of a parrot regulated by the Washington Convention, Appendix I, the buyer must confirm that the seller obtained the bird legally; that is, he must be able to verify the ownership of the animal through the presentation of an official certificate. Should the parrot have been obtained before the Washington Convention or the Addendum to the Washington Convention went into effect, then the owner is subsequently obligated to allow the authorities to verify the legality of the purchase of the parrot.

Every parrot fancier should strictly observe the legislated regulations, since the birds could be confiscated by the empowered governmental authorities if the Washington Convention for the protection of species is violated.

Top: The Green-cheeked Amazon, *Amazona viridigenalis,* is sometimes called the Red-crowned Parrot.

Bottom: Because of its reputation as a talker, the Yellow-naped Amazon, *Amazona ochrocephala auropalliata,* is very attractive to smugglers.

The parrot known as the Yellow-naped Amazon is a form of *Amazona ochrocephala,* the Yellow-crowned Amazon, bearing the subspecific name *auropalliata.* Some taxonomists have concluded that this parrot now deserves specific status, with the name *Amazona auropalliata.*

The Systematic Position of the Amazon Parrots

Parrots, with their approximately 328 species, constitute a clearly demarcated order in the large class Aves that shows no kindred relationship to other orders of birds. In the interest of greater clarity, the concepts should first be explained in more detail.

All of the approximately 8600 to 8800 species of birds, from the hummingbird to the Ostrich, are warm-blooded vertebrates, and are subsumed in class Aves (birds). The class is made up of the various orders (for example, parrots constitute one order). The different classifications seeking to represent the hereditary relationships among birds of course have the result that the birds are arranged differently. Wolters arrives at 50 orders of birds in his recently published systematics; Wetmore, who condensed the entire system, employs only 26 orders.

The next lower level of classification is the family, which is made up of subfamilies. The subfamily consists of one or more genera. The genus is made up of very closely related species. The individual species does not, however, represent the final link in the long chain, since in many species the geographic races constitute subspecies.

For example: The placement of the Panama Amazon (*Amazona ochrocephala panamensis*) in the system of classification: class—Aves; order—Psittaciformes; family—Psittacidae; subfamily—Psittacinae; genus—*Amazona*; species—*Amazona ochrocephala*; subspecies: *Amazona ochrocephala panamensis*.

New findings and empirical data necessarily require that changes be made to the existing standards and systems; accordingly, what it published today can be totally out of date tomorrow.

In the opinion of the author, the systematics proposed by J. L. Peters represents, at least for parrots, the foundation, or, as the case may be, the cornerstone for any system of classification. In this system, the origin of parrots, which certainly should be sought in the region of New Guinea and northeastern Australia, is clearly set forth. The author sees the primitive parrot forms still living today in the Kakapo (*Strigops habroptilus*), the Keas (*Nestor*), the Pesquet's Parrot (*Psittrichas fulgidus*), and possibly the Palm Cockatoo (*Probosciger aterrimus*). To be sure, Dr. J. Steinbacher points

The Panama Amazon is placed in the subspecies *Amazona ochrocephala panamensis*. All amazons belong to the class Aves, the order Psittaciformes, the family Psittacidae, the subfamily Psittacinae and the genus *Amazona*.

Top: The Yellow-faced Amazon, *Amazona xanthops*, as a youngster. The author regards the status of this amazon as questionable; although little is known about its life in the wild, its observed behavior and diet distinguish it from the other 27 species of the genus.
Below: Members of a closely related genus (*Pionites*) are these White-bellied Caiques, *Pionites l eucogaster*, South American parrots.
Opposite: Pesquet's Parrot, *Psittrichas fulgidus*, represents a living expression of the parrot in its more primitive form.

out that these forms are not necessarily ancient, tertiary forms; on the contrary, it is entirely possible that secondary retrogressive evolution has occurred here, as is the case, for example, with the Ostrich (*Struthio camelus*), which had flying ancestors and is today no longer considered to be a primitive species.

Amazon parrots are, with one exception, a clearly delimited genus consisting of 27 species. In the opinion of the author, the Yellow-faced Amazon, *Amazona xanthops*, cannot be considered a member of this group with certainty. Its behavioral traits, along with the dietary items consumed by the bird, clearly separate it from the habits of the other species. This should be qualified, however, by pointing out that only very scanty reports about this species' life in the wild exist. It can be assumed that in the near future, after a few Yellow-faced Amazons have been kept by breeders, it will be possible to investigate the relationship of this amazon to the other species of the genus more thoroughly. At the very least, it will be possible to collect information on its feeding, drinking, courtship, and breeding habits, which will then allow one conclusion or

another to be reached. At the moment, the author sees in the Yellow-faced Amazon a link connecting the genera *Amazona* with *Pionopsitta*, or *Gypopsitta* and *Hapalopsittaca*, or both. Another very closely related genus is *Pionus*, with its eight (?) species.

At present, nothing much can be said about which group the origin of the American parrots should be sought in, but one can possibly proceed from the supposition that the present variety of forms evolved from the short-tailed parrots (Psittacini), a group in the subfamily Psittacinae, for which the original locality was limited to Madagascar and Africa. The present African genera *Coracopsis*, *Psittacus*, and *Poicephalus* may therefore have evolved much earlier and so are very likely the ancestors of the New World parrots.

Amazon parrots have evolved into many species; geographical considerations suggest that they

Amazona aestiva, the Blue-fronted Amazon, is purported by the author to be among the closest links to the "primal" amazons.

originated in present-day northeastern Brazil. The surviving species *Amazona amazonica* and *Amazona aestiva* are probably most like the "primal" amazon parrot and may be very closely connected in their evolutionary history to this ancient form. The Blue-fronted Amazon (*A. aestiva*), with its extremely variable coloration and the often extreme difference in size between individuals, shows that if groups of individuals become geographically isolated from other members of the species, new subspecies could evolve relatively quickly, and new species could possibly also be expected after only a few generations. The remaining 25 species could have evolved from the two previously mentioned species or already extinct species over the course

of millennia. Through particular behavioral traits, and also through differences in plumage characteristics between species, it is apparent that the evolutionary phases began and ended at different times. In part, the processes are still in full swing: in several forms, the evolution of new species, such as the Tucuman Amazon, can be discerned. Certainly, a number of forms intermediate between the present-day species became extinct in the past, so that the evolutionary relationships between the surviving forms cannot be clearly reconstructed. At the same time, however, it can be recognized that the demarcation between several species is not complete, and that one could certainly also speak of geographic forms, such as *Amazona ventralis*, as *Amazona leucocephala ventralis*. A similar situation also applies to *Amazona arausiaca* with *A. versicolor*; *Amazona brasiliensis* with *A. rhodocorytha* and *A. dufresniana*, and also to *Amazona finschi* with *A. viridigenalis*, and so on.

What follows is a listing of the species groups with their respective species and subspecies, derived from J. L. Peters, *Checklist of Birds of the World* and H. E. Wolters, *Systematische Liste der Vogelarten der Erde* ('Systematic List of the Bird Species of the World'), which the author has based on findings collected in the last two decades, such as behavioral traits of the different species in captivity, and also the geographic ranges and plumage characters. The following list of all amazon-parrot species, including subspecies, cannot, of course, be considered a definitive classification. Many points must still be pursued and resolved; thus, for example, it is still open to question whether *Amazona mercenaria* can properly be considered a separate species, or if it is possibly only the "montane form" of *Amazona farinosa*.

Pionites melanocephala, the Black-headed Caique, is a member of a genus the author sees as closely related to the amazons, notably the Yellow-faced Amazon, *Amazona xanthops.*

1ST SPECIES GROUP
1. *Amazona amazonica*
   A. amazonica amazonica
   A. amazonica tobagensis
2. *Amazona aestiva*
   A. aestiva aestiva
   A. aestiva xanthopteryx

2ND SPECIES GROUP
3. *Amazona ochrocephala*
   A. ochrocephala ochrocephala
   A. ochrocephala xantholaema
   A. ochrocephala nattereri
   A. ochrocephala panamensis
   A. ochrocephala auropalliata
   A. ochrocephala parvipes
   A. ochrocephala belizensis
   A. ochrocephala oratrix
   A. ochrocephala tresmariae
4. *Amazona barbadensis*
   A. barbadensis barbadensis
   A. barbadensis rothschildi
5. *Amazona farinosa*
   A. farinosa farinosa
   A. farinosa inornata
   A. farinosa chapmani
   A. farinosa virenticeps
   A. farinosa guatemalae
6. *Amazona mercenaria*
   A. mercenaria mercenaria
   A. mercenaria canipalliata

3RD SPECIES GROUP
7. *Amazona finschi*
   A. finschi finschi
   A. finschi woodi
8. *Amazona viridigenalis*
9. *Amazona autumnalis*
   A. autumnalis autumnalis
   A. autumnalis salvini
   A. autumnalis lilacina
10. *Amazona diadema*

4TH SPECIES GROUP
11. *Amazona festiva*
   A. festiva festiva
   A. festiva bodini

5TH SPECIES GROUP
12. *Amazona brasiliensis*
13. *Amazona rhodocorytha*
14. *Amazona dufresniana*

6TH SPECIES GROUP
15. *Amazona vinacea*

7TH SPECIES GROUP
16. *Amazona pretrei*
   A. pretrei pretrei
   A. pretrei tucumana

8TH SPECIES GROUP
17. *Amazona albifrons*
   A. albifrons albifrons
   A. albifrons saltuensis
   A. albifrons nana
   A. albifrons xantholora
18. *Amazona leucocephala*
   A. leucocephala leucocephala
   A. leucocephala palmarum
   A. leucocephala caymanensis
   A. leucocephala hesterna
   A. leucocephala bahamensis
19. *Amazona ventralis*
20. *Amazona collaria*
21. *Amazona vittata*
   A. vittata vittata
   A. vittata gracilipes †
22. *Amazona agilis*

9TH SPECIES GROUP
23. *Amazona arausiaca*
24. *Amazona versicolor*
   Amazona violacea †
   Amazona martinica †
25. *Amazona imperialis*

10TH SPECIES GROUP
26. *Amazona guildingii*

11TH SPECIES GROUP
27. *Amazona xanthops*

The system favored by the author does not differ substantially from the list advanced by James Lee Peters. Peters's system, however, requires minor corrections with respect to the formation of groups within the taxa, and also a modification to take into account the most recent findings with respect to the species and subspecies. The primary changes should be briefly listed once again: *Amazona diadema*, formerly *Amazona autumnalis diadema; Amazona rhodocorytha*, formerly *Amazona dufresniana rhodocorytha; Amazona dufresniana*, formerly *Amazona dufresniana dufresniana; Amazona*

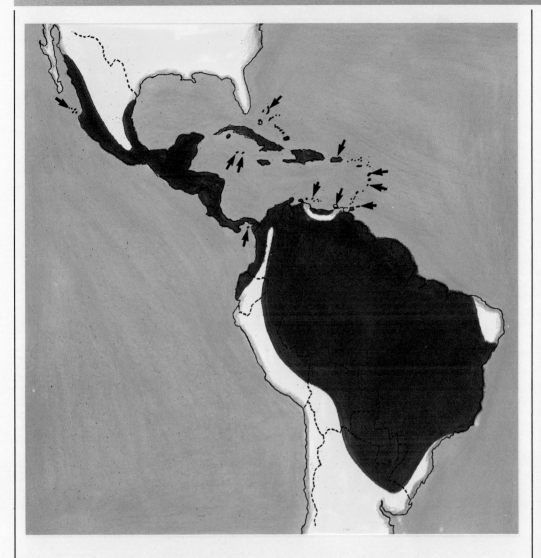

Distribution of the genus *Amazona*.

albifrons xantholora, formerly *Amazona xantholora*.

With these changes, the arrangement proposed by J. L. Peters, which is published below, will continue to be valid; scientific institutions support this treatment almost exclusively.

1. *Amazona collaria* (4 subspecies)
2. *Amazona leucocephala*
3. *Amazona ventralis*
4. *Amazona xantholora*
5. *Amazona albifrons* (3 subspecies)
6. *Amazona agilis*
7. *Amazona vittata* (2 subspecies)
8. *Amazona pretrei* (2 subspecies)
9. *Amazona viridigenalis*
10. *Amazona finschi*
11. *Amazona autumnalis* (4 subspecies)
12. *Amazona dufresniana* (2 subspecies)
13. *Amazona brasiliensis*
14. *Amazona arausiaca*
15. *Amazona festiva* (2 subspecies)
16. *Amazona xanthops*
17. *Amazona barbadensis* (2 subspecies)
18. *Amazona aestiva* 2 subspecies)
19. *Amazona ochrocephala* (7 subspecies)
20. *Amazona amazonica* (2 subspecies)
21. *Amazona mercenaria* (2 subspecies)
22. *Amazona farinosa* (4 subspecies)
23. *Amazona vinacea*
24. *Amazona guildingii*
25. *Amazona versicolor*
26. *Amazona imperialis*
    Psittacus violaceus †
    Amazona martinica †

Top: Amazona ventralis, the Hispaniolan Amazon, resides in the Dominican Republic and Haiti; alternatively, this bird is known as the Santo Domingo Amazon.
Bottom left: The author was able to purchase this unusually colored amazon parrot in Mexico. A year later the bird developed into a completely normally colored Lilac-crowned Amazon, *Amazona finschii finschii*.
Bottom right: The Lilac-crowned Amazon, *Amazona finschii finschii*, courting Vinaceous Amazon, *Amazona vinacea*.

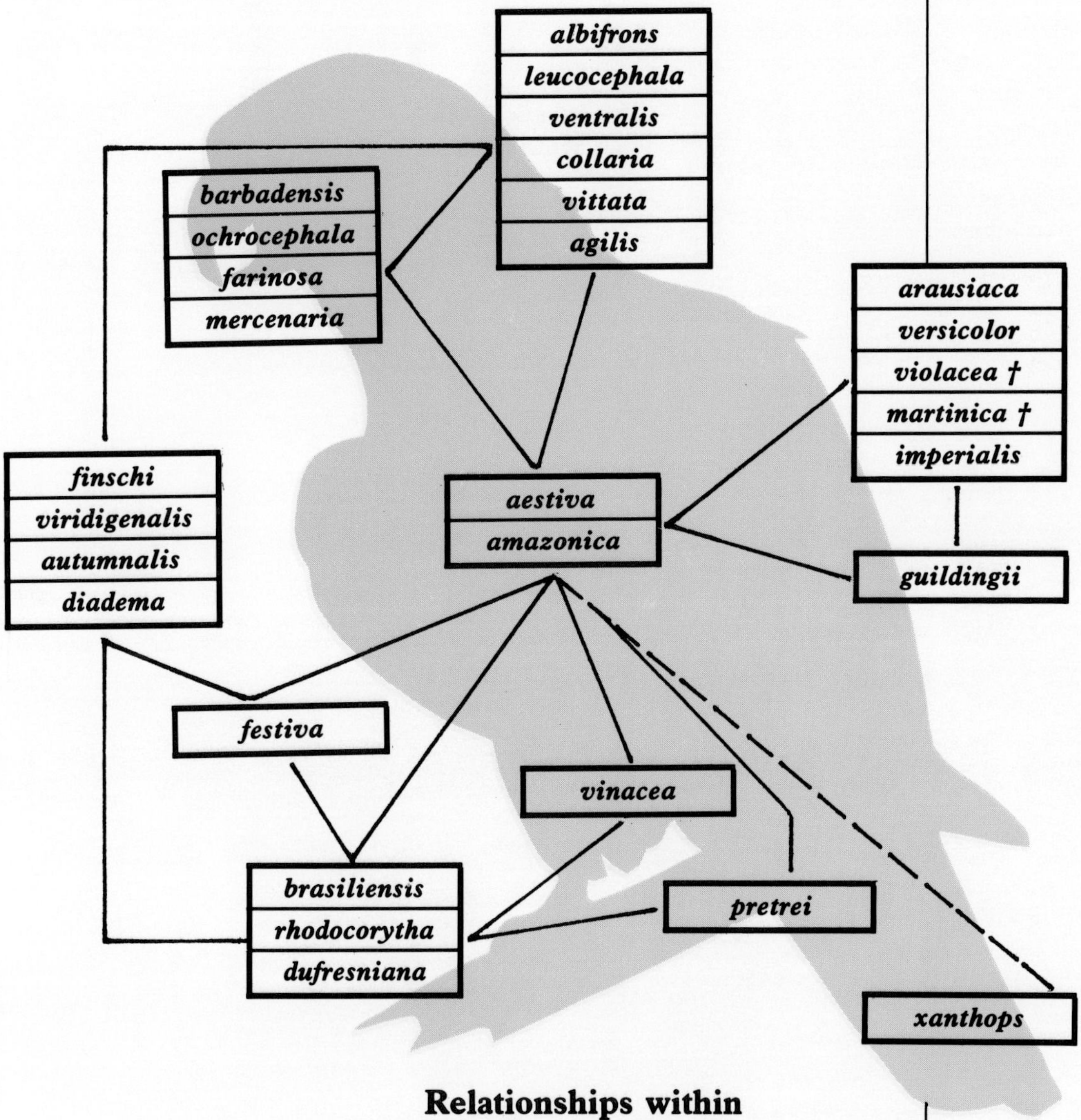

**Relationships within
the Genus *Amazona***
(according to Hoppe)

The diagram shows the following groups:

albifrons / *leucocephala* / *ventralis* / *collaria* / *vittata* / *agilis*

barbadensis / *ochrocephala* / *farinosa* / *mercenaria*

arausiaca / *versicolor* / *violacea †* / *martinica †* / *imperialis*

guildingii

finschi / *viridigenalis* / *autumnalis* / *diadema*

aestiva / *amazonica*

festiva

vinacea

brasiliensis / *rhodocorytha* / *dufresniana*

pretrei

xanthops

Anatomy of the amazon parrot.

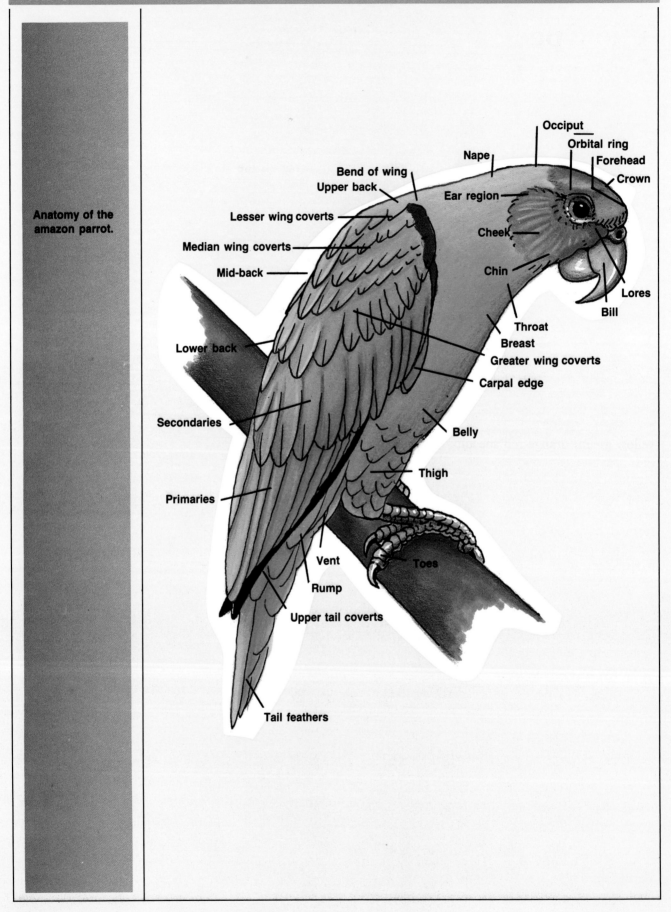

Occiput

Orbital ring

Forehead

Crown

Nape

Ear region

Bend of wing

Upper back

Cheek

Lesser wing coverts

Chin

Lores

Median wing coverts

Bill

Mid-back

Throat

Breast

Greater wing coverts

Lower back

Carpal edge

Belly

Secondaries

Thigh

Primaries

Vent

Toes

Rump

Upper tail coverts

Tail feathers

The Species of Amazon Parrots

Orange-winged Amazon
Amazona amazonica (Linnaeus)
1766 — 2 (3) subspecies

1. *Amazona amazonica amazonica* (Linnaeus)

DESCRIPTION: Length approximately 32 cm.; green; nape and upper back has dark edging; yellow on crown and cheeks; crown also blue with a narrow yellow frontal band; blue above the eye and on the lores; throat yellow green; ear coverts darker green; carpal edge yellow green; orange-red speculum on the three outer secondaries; the first secondaries dark blue at the tips; undersides of wings lighter green; tail feathers green; the outer four tail feathers have red on the inner vanes; iris orange; orbital ring gray; bill dark horn color; upper mandible changing from gray to black toward the tip; legs gray.

RANGE: From northeastern Colombia through eastern Ecuador and eastern Peru east to the Brazilian states of Paraná and Rio de Janeiro; French Guiana, Surinam, Guyana, and Venezuela.

2. *Amazona amazonica tobagensis* Cory

DESCRIPTION: Like the nominate subspecies, but somewhat larger with orangish red speculum extending over four feathers.
RANGE: The islands of Trinidad and Tobago.

3. *Amazona amazonica micra* (Griscom and Greenway)

This so-called subspecies, which occurs in Surinam, should be synonymized with the nominate form.

REMARKS: The author has chosen a new German name for the 'Venezuelan Amazon,' the range of which is not limited to Venezuela, but, on the contrary, is spread over a large area of South America. In imitation of the English name, Orange-winged Amazon, it is given the name *Orangeflügel-Amazone*.
WAY OF LIFE: The Orange-winged

The Orange-winged Amazon, *Amazona amazonica*, is principally green, with its name-giving orange coloration on its three outer secondary feathers. Yellow coloration persists on the crown and cheeks, blue above the eyes and the narrow frontal band.

The island of Tobago: tropical coastal rain forest as encountered in many of the coastal regions of Central and South America.

Amazon, *Amazona amazonica amazonica*, is found throughout a very large region. It appears to be the most abundant of the larger species of parrots in Guyana and French Guiana. In the evening, many thousands of amazon parrots can be observed on their roosting trees in the mangrove swamps. The large flocks split up in the morning, and the birds then go in pairs or in very small parties, possibly

family groups (?), in search of food.

In Guyana, Orange-winged Amazons apparently favor to a considerable extent damp forested coastal zones and mangrove-swamp areas. These amazons are also quite abundant in Venezuela and can frequently be observed in the same areas as the Yellow-crowned Amazon (*Amazona ochrocephala ochrocephala*), but here too the Orange-winged Amazons apparently also favor the wetter forests (in contrast, one

finds the Yellow-crowned Amazon more often in the dry forests). Dr. Sick reports that in the winter months Orange-winged Amazons migrate together with Red-browed Amazons (*A. rhodocorytha*) through the mangrove swamps in the Brazilian coastal states of southeast Bahia to northeast Rio de Janeiro. In Ecuador, Peru, Bolivia, and in the Mato Grosso of Brazil, these amazon parrots were also encountered at higher elevations but are not nearly as abundant there as in the coastal regions. In Colombia they inhabit the tropical lowlands of the eastern slopes of the Andes. In northern Colombia, Orange-winged Amazons are again more abundant in the swampy regions of the Rio Magdalena. Swampy regions with stands of mangroves are the habitats favored by the amazon parrots. Forshaw (1971) reports that in the vicinity of Georgetown, Guyana, he observed many thousands of Orange-winged Amazons alight on a large stand of bamboo in the middle of an abandoned farm on the Demerara River. From late afternoon until darkness fell, new groups, pairs, or flocks continually flew to their roosting sites. When they flew by, he could also identify Mealy Amazons (*Amazona farinosa*). Parrots that flew in from across the river almost always congregated in a large deciduous tree near the bank and stopped there to perform their antic behaviors. Forshaw repeatedly saw screeching birds beating their wings wildly, while they hung head down and only held on to the branch with one foot. There were so many parrots that the large bamboo stalks bent under the weight of the birds. The effect produced by this immense congregation was strengthened by the continuous screeching, which rose to a deafening level of noise.

Feeding takes place in the morning and afternoon hours. During the hot

hours around noon, the birds rest in the high treetops. Preferred foods are the fruits, nuts, berries, buds, and seeds that grow on tall trees. The birds go near or onto the ground only reluctantly.

The breeding season of the Orange-winged Amazon occurs in the northern part of their range in the months from February till June, and on Tobago continues into August. McLoughlin reports (*Foreign Birds*, 1970) that in Guyana he found a 1.6-meter-deep cavity with three young at a height of about 16 m. in a dead tree. Two chicks were almost fully fledged, but the third

Amazona amazonica is among the most frequently kept amazon parrots, along with *A. ochrocephala* and *A. aestiva*. These amazons have all done extremely well in captivity and presently do not face the danger of extinction.

youngster was considerably smaller and very sparsely feathered.

On several occasions the author was able to visit the localities on Trinidad and Tobago where *Amazona amazonica tobagensis* is found. On Trinidad in particular, the western coastal and low-lying areas are quite densely populated and are being used for agriculture to a greater extent. The upland region, the Northern Range, in the northern part of the island reaches elevations of up to 941 m. in the Cerro del Aripo, and is sparsely inhabited. The Central Range and the Southern Range are hilly country with an elevation of up to 300 m., which are little used for agriculture and therefore still covered with relatively dense woodlands. The Orange-winged Amazon on Trinidad is found in the regions referred to, as well as in the mangrove swamps in the coastal zones. On Tobago these amazon parrots occur in the eastern part of the island around the towering range of mountains, the Main Ridge, which is also covered with dense rain and montane forests.

Outside of the breeding season these amazons form flocks of up to a hundred birds, in which they join with the Yellow-crowned Amazon (*Amazona ochrocephala ochrocephala*) on Trinidad. The breeding season occurs in the so-called dry season: February (occasionally January) until June, on Tobago sometimes lasting until August. The nest cavities are usually located in dead palms starting at a height of about 6 m. Because of the dense foliage, the nest sites are not easily detected and, therefore, not frequently cited in the literature. Up to five white eggs (size approximately 42.3 × 29.7 mm.) are laid. Richard French as well as Nottebohm and Nottebohm state an incubation period of three weeks and a nestling period of two months. This

Distribution of *Amazona amazonica*.

must certainly be a mistake. With Orange-winged Amazons kept in captivity, incubation lasted 25–26 days and the nestling period of the young about three months.

On Trinidad the author had the opportunity to examine about 15 amazon parrots kept by bird dealers and fanciers, and determined from ten birds which were examined more closely that in seven parrots the red speculum extended over only three feathers, as with the nominate form. In the remaining three Orange-winged Amazons, the speculum extended over four feathers. Possibly both subspecies are found on Trinidad. This would be in no way remarkable since the South American mainland is located only about 8 km. from the northwestern part of Trinidad and can be reached by the birds at any time.

One bird dealer living on Trinidad told the author that he purchased about 100 Orange-winged Amazons in Guyana for an export firm. When the export did not take place (the American customer had canceled his order), he released about 80% of the "Guyana" birds. These released birds could certainly have become well established on Trinidad. The incident was said to have occurred in 1970 or 1971. To what extent the difference between the subspecies (the speculum) has been retained, given interbreeding

Opposite: Portrait of the Orange-winged Amazon. The appeal of this amazon is not reliant on its handsome appearance alone, as the species is well mannered and easily trained.

between the nominate and the *tobagensis* forms, is not known to the author.

In the Botanical Garden on the north edge of the capital, Port of Spain, the author could regularly observe the arrival of flocks, presumably family groups, in the afternoon hours. The amazon parrots flew to palms heavily laden with fruit and ate their fill. After landing and even while feeding they were very difficult to detect, since they were completely silent during those times. When flying they make an unbelievable amount of noise and can be located without difficulty even at great distances.

They are not as abundant on Tobago (last visit 1979); here only one pair and a small family group of six birds could be located. In previous years the author was able to observe many more animals.

Orange-winged Amazons are certainly not yet endangered, but through the continuing settlement and clearing of large areas of South America, they too are being extirpated more and more.

CARE AND BREEDING: The Orange-winged Amazon is, along with the Yellow-crowned and Blue-fronted amazons, the most frequently kept species. In any zoological garden several specimens are usually on exhibit. They are constantly available in the animal trade. Although the Orange-winged Amazon is present in Europe in large numbers, successful propagation is very rare.

The author was able to purchase a guaranteed pair of Orange-winged Amazons from a fancier in Trinidad in 1976. The animals were captured several years before in Chaquaramas, in the extreme northwestern part of the island. Although the birds came from Trinidad, and thus belonged to the subspecies *Amazona amazonica tobagensis*, the red speculum only

extended over three feathers. The amazon parrots were kept in an indoor flight of approximately eight cubic meters. In the Spring of 1978, the author happened to be away on an extended study trip. The bird collection, including the Orange-winged Amazons, were lovingly cared for by a neighbor's wife during this time. Upon the author's return, she reported that only one Orange-winged Amazon could still be seen; the second remained inside the tree trunk continuously. An ill-advised nest inspection which was undertaken immediately showed a dead egg (size, 38.2 × 28.9 mm.) and a youngster about seven weeks old. Since the amazon-parrot pair had had many weeks without the slightest disturbance, the nest inspection threw them so out of balance that from that time on they paid no more attention to the youngster—a clear example of how sensitively they react to disturbances during the breeding period. The young amazon parrot was subsequently removed from the nest and raised by hand. At the start of hand rearing the young amazon parrot was already relatively well feathered. The tail feathers were about one cm. long, the wing feathers were already well developed, and the first feather sheaths had appeared on the head; the bill was dark gray with horn-colored spots; the eyes were very large and conspicuous with almost black irises. The dark, almost black legs were almost as large as those of the adult birds.

The little Orange-winged Amazon was placed in a small raffia basket padded with ample paper fleece. At first, it was fed about five times a day; this cycle was reduced to two daily feedings by an age of about four months. The most varied kinds of baby food (manufactured by Alete) were used. The prepared pap was warmed to body temperature and fortified with all

A young Orange-winged Amazon. These parrots begin flight attempts at about 80–85 days of age and are quickly acclimated to the perch and hand.

kinds of rolled oats, corn flakes, wheat bran, banana, white bread, mashed egg yolk, all types of fruit, and a bit of edible calcium in powdered form. Once the youngster opened its bill promptly, the feeding could be done without difficulty. As soon as the young amazon parrot saw one's little finger, which had been dipped in the thick pap, it opened its bill wide, and made swallowing movements at the first finger-bill contact. It could consume unbelievable amounts at every feeding, and the crop bulged considerably. On the second day after separation from the parents, the little parrot already perched on the rim of the raffia basket, and two days later it tried to walk for the first time. The first attempts to fly took place when it was about 80–85 days old. At this time it also raised its

voice for the first time, and it was observed with dismay that the juvenile could screech even louder than the adults. At the slightest noise it was inclined to to start screeching immediately.

In 1978, a German bird fancier (Mitterhuber and de Grahl 1979) was able to breed Orange-winged Amazons. The birds started to feed each other at the beginning of May. On the first of June, an egg already lay in the nest box. A 50-liter wine barrel, placed at a height of about 2.50 m., served the birds as a nest cavity. Two additional eggs were laid, and an inspection revealed three fertilized eggs. On the 28th of May the first faint peeping could be heard coming from the nest box. Upon examination, which was only possible ten days later, two chicks were observed. The third egg had been fertile but had died. The youngsters' eyes were open very slightly. The plumage was still quite sparse: only a few gray down feathers. The eyes opened completely after three weeks of life. The wing feathers broke through in the sixth week of life. After eight weeks the first yellowish feathers were visible on the head; the tips of the wing feathers were likewise clearly yellow. After about ten weeks the two parrots were almost fully feathered, and apparently already exhibited recognizable sex differences in the plumage, similar to that of parents. In the breeding pair, the male had a more stocky head and bill and more pronounced blue feather markings. In the female, the yellow was more extensive, particularly in cheek area.

How long the nestling period lasted and at what age the juveniles attained complete independence, the author was not able to ascertain.

The first breeding of the Orange-winged Amazon, at that time still known as *Psittacus amazonicus*, apparently occurred in Rome in 1801. In Tampa, three young were raised by hand in 1970.

Several yellow Orange-winged Amazons have already been sighted in the wild. At the Taington Zoo in Great Britain, a yellow variety of this amazon parrot species was on exhibit in 1960.

Choosing the right accommodations for the amazon parrots requires time, commitment and study. The habits of these birds in the wild reveal much about their care. This owner has provided tropical fruit-tree branches in the cage for the bird's consumption. It is vital to know which fruits and branches should and should not be provided to your parrot.

Blue-fronted Amazon
Amazona aestiva (Linnaeus) 1758 —
2 subspecies

Named for the blue coloration of its forehead and lores, *Amazona aestiva* is a native inhabitant of east-central Brazil.

1. *Amazona aestiva aestiva* (Linnaeus)

DESCRIPTION: Length approximately 37 cm.; green, with dark edging; forehead and lores blue; crown, eye region, cheeks, and throat yellow; bend of wing red, often with yellow interspersed; primaries and secondaries green, blue only toward the tips; red speculum on the five outer secondaries; undersides of wing blue green; tail feathers green with yellowish green tips; outer tail feathers red at the base; thighs yellowish green; iris orange; orbital ring grayish; bill grayish black; legs gray.

Youngsters: Yellow and blue areas on the head less extensive; iris dark brown.

RANGE: East-central Brazil from Piauí south to Rio Grande do Sul and southwest to the Mato Grosso.

2. *Amazona aestiva xanthopteryx* (Berlepsch) 1896 — Yellow-winged Amazon

DESCRIPTION: Like the nominate subspecies, but with yellow on the bend of the wing; carpal edge yellow.

RANGE: From southwestern Mato Grosso in Brazil through Paraguay to northern Buenos Aires in Argentina.

REMARKS: Graf Berlepsch described the second subspecies of the Blue-fronted Amazon in 1896 in *Ornithologische Monatsberichte*, 4, p. 173. Apparently the specimen which was collected by G. Garlepp on 29 December 1889 in Bueyes, Bolivia (No. 387 in the collection of G. Garlepp) was available to him (J. Steinbacher 1962, *Beiträge zur Kenntnis der Vögel von Paraguay*, pp. 49–50). The type specimen has a yellow bend of the wing and carpal edge, but also exhibits isolated red feathers in the carpal edge. Dr. A. Laubmann 1930 (*Wissenschaftliche Ergebnisse der Deutschen Gran Chaco-Expedition—Vögel*, pp. 119–120) and 1939 (*Die Vögel von Paraguay*, Volume 1, pp. 186–187), as well as Dr. J. Steinbacher 1962, have already pointed out a discrepancy in the 'Berlepschian race' *xanthopteryx*.

My examination of all specimens of *Amazona aestiva* in the Stuttgart and Frankfurt museums, as well as my inspection of many living specimens, indicates that this species exhibits an extremely variable coloration in the plumage of the head, breast, and bend of the wing, in which *A. a. aestiva* and *A. a. xanthopteryx* both exhibit the variability to the same degree. Typical specimens with a pure red or yellow—as the case may be—bend of the wing and carpal edge occur very rarely. It should be noted that the Brazilian animals, that is the so-called nominate form, exhibit a more extensive area of red or yellow-red coloration on the bend of the wing or the carpal edge, and that in *A. a. xanthopteryx*, as a rule, the yellow component is predominant. The color transition takes place over an extremely large area and cannot be demarcated. A similar situation occurs with the difference in size. The northern and eastern forms are smaller than the western and southern forms, but at the same time it can be demonstrated that within small areas of the range large size differences exist between individuals. On the basis of all the characters used for systematic determination, the subspecies *Amazona aestiva xanthopteryx* (Berlepsch) 1896 would no longer be considered valid. The correct designation should read: *Amazona aestiva* (Linnaeus) 1758 [*Psittacus aestivus* Linnaeus, *Syst. Nat.* X, 1; p. 101 (1758 — America: terra typica subst.: southern Brazil)].

WAY OF LIFE: The Blue-fronted Amazon is a typical inhabitant of tropical dry forests, savannas, and palm groves, and shows partiality to valleys formed by water courses and to

With many hardy specimens accessible to the bird fancy, the Blue-fronted Amazon sustains a high level of popularity among the amazon parrots.

The Blue-fronted Amazon, *Amazona aestiva*, exhibits extremely variable plumage coloration; in the same way, noticeable differences in the sizes of individuals are recognized.

swampy regions. As is true of virtually all species of neotropical parrots, Blue-fronted Amazons assemble in family groups and small flocks outside the breeding season. In the evening hours, the small groups congregate at roosting trees, which are used for weeks and months at a time. Parties continue to fly to the communal roosting sites from all directions even after nightfall. Gatherings of more than a thousand individuals are not a rarity. The competition for the best roosting sites, of course, often leads to fights, which are then carried out with the loudest screeching imaginable. As soon as quiet has been restored, it does not take long until a newly arrived party again causes a great commotion among the community already assembled. One can observe similar spectacles in Central Europe at the roosting sites of the European Starling (*Sturnus vulgaris*) in summer, after their breeding season. At first light, the amazon parrots' importunate concert of calls begins; since the calls each bird delivers are extremely loud, and because of the large number of individuals, the chorus swells to a deafening din. The typical call of the Blue-fronted Amazon is comparable to the baying of a dog, and sounds something like *paupau paupau*. The screeching phase is interrupted by diligent preening, and about an hour after dawn the departure in small groups takes place. Mated pairs fly close together, side by side or one over the other.

The fruits of different species of palms in half-ripe and ripe condition constitute the principal part of the diet of Blue-fronted Amazons. In particular, the fruits of the *Mauritia* species, which bear fruit at the most varied times in the same habitat, provide a constant food supply in a large part of the range. The parrots, however, also take other fruits and berries, as well as leaf and flower buds. One can gather from some of the literature that Blue-fronted Amazons invade agricultural areas and inflict great damage on corn and grain fields. These remarks amount to generalizations of no value. As is true of most amazon-parrot species, the Blue-fronted Amazon does not go down to the ground or near it. In this regard, this species, along with other neotropical parrots, differs from the majority of parakeets. Even when feeding in trees, amazon parrots exploit food sources in the canopy. They only come down to the ground to drink and to take in mineral-rich soil; in so doing, they act extremely cautiously. J. Ungersen (Steinbacher 1962), who collected specimens in Paraguay for various American and German natural-history museums over many years, says this about the Blue-fronted Amazons indigenous there: "This is the only parrot which causes no harm to the farmer. He lives on the fruits of the forest. In the months of May, June,

Distribution of the two *Amazona aestiva* subspecies: (1) *A. a. aestiva*; (2) *A. a. xanthopteryx.*

and July, he migrates into eastern Paraguay. One is glad to keep him on farms, since he is extraordinarily clever, and learns to talk and sing songs. He nests once a year and has two to three eggs." Many more testimonials exist to indicate that the Blue-fronted Amazon, as well as a number of other amazon-parrot species, never invade grain fields and cause damage there.

The Blue-fronted Amazon, like other parrot species, follows a daily routine. After the morning calling-and-preening phase, which lasts about an hour, the flight from the roosting sites to the watering holes takes place. After that, the feeding sites, which are often twenty to thirty kilometers from the roosting sites, are visited. The birds, moving in small groups, remain at the feeding sites until the afternoon hours. At noon, feeding is interrupted by an extensive preening and resting phase, in which it can be clearly noted that the pairs perch close together and undertake the activities simultaneously. Before the return to the roosting sites, the birds again feed extensively, and they usually fly to the watering places once more to drink. All flight activities are accompanied by the loudest possible noise; that is, the birds constantly call while in flight. Mated pairs always fly close together.

The breeding season of the Blue-

The species prefers broken palms and empty tree cavities at high altitudes for breeding sites.

fronted Amazon is synchronized with the rainy season. It begins around October in the southernmost part of the range, and in the North shifts to as late as the beginning of December. Blue-fronted Amazons, like most parrot species, are monogamous, which is to say that they mate for life. Courtship behavior, therefore, is not particularly pronounced, and the particular courtship rituals are doubtless only a stimulating factor in reproduction. The cocks parade with slightly drooping wings and spread tail feathers, so that the red markings take full effect. The females react to the males' courtship quite indifferently, but immediately allow themselves to be fed when the cock regurgitates food. In so doing, they crouch down and tuck their head back so that the bill points upward. The cock encloses the right corner of the hen's bill from above and delivers the food. Copulation is performed with the birds perched next to each other, whereby the birds hold

on with the toes of the touching side and rub their cloacas against one another. Soon after the start of the courtship season the birds abandon their group life and leave the flock in pairs. Adult animals without mates and juvenile amazon parrots that are not yet sexually mature remain behind in the group. To what extent old breeding pairs return to old breeding territories which were already used in previous years has not yet been sufficiently studied. On the strength of my observations in the wild of the Orange-winged Amazon (*Amazona amazonica*), which after all has a similar breeding behavior, I can state that a breeding pair of amazon parrots requires an area of six to eight square kilometers during the breeding period. Undoubtedly, the amount of space required is determined by the food supply available in the particular territory, but an area of six to ten square kilometers, as a rule, would seem to be the space required. As breeding sites, tree cavities high up in dead trees or broken-off palms are favored. As a rule, the hens lay two or three eggs and begin incubation immediately after the first egg is laid. Incubation is performed by the female. The male watches over the nest cavity during the incubation period, and also provides his mate with food. The female usually leaves the nest site only once a day in order to evacuate and drink. After an incubation period of 26 days the chicks hatch at the intervals in which the eggs were laid (two days). In the first days of life, the cock continues to feed the female, and she passes the food on to the young. Only after about eight days does the mother bird leave the young and take part in the search for food. At this time the direct feeding of the young by the cock begins. The nestling period lasts about 60 days. After the young leave the nest, the family group still stays close together for a fairly long time. Especially during

Amazona aestiva xanthopteryx is similar to the nominate subspecies excepting its yellow wing bends and yellow carpal edge. Its range extends from southwestern Mato Grosso (Brazil) through Paraguay to northern Buenos Aires (Argentina).

CARE AND BREEDING: The Blue-fronted Amazon, along with the Grey Parrot (*Psittacus erithacus*) and several subspecies of the Yellow-crowned Amazon (*Amazona ochrocephala*), is one of the most popular parrots among bird fanciers. Even today, the Blue-fronted Amazon is one of the amazon-parrot species that is regularly imported. Unfortunately, the majority of the imported birds, virtually all of which are specimens from Paraguay and Bolivia, are in the hands of owners who keep them as pets isolated in their cages. At the same time, a trend toward keeping them in pairs can be recognized, and this state of affairs is all the more encouraging because in recent years many breeding pairs have been put together. Several reports in the specialty literature of successful propagation of the Blue-fronted Amazon render it superfluous to discuss the course of breeding in detail. Therefore, in the following I mention only a few details which are worth knowing in case of an expected breeding:

Sexual maturity: occurs an age of three to five years. Sex differences: none; endoscopy is recommended. Accommodations: a flight if possible; if breeding is desired, keeping them with other parrots is not advisable. Reproductive season: one can promote reproduction artificially through climatic conditions and feeding practices, thereby bringing the mates into breeding condition simultaneously. Courtship period: about two to three weeks. Clutch: two or three eggs. Egg size: about 38 × 30 mm. Incubation period: about 26 days. Nestling period: about 60 days. Independence: the young are completely self-sufficient at an age of about four months, but should be left with the adults as long as possible, possibly until the start of the next breeding season.

the first months of life, the young amazon parrots are exposed to many dangers—harpy-eagles and falcons often successfully capture juveniles. Some time later the family group is integrated into the flock.

Opposite: The Blue-fronted Amazon reaches sexual maturity between the ages of three and five years. This handsome bird appears to be a hardy, mature specimen of the species.

A youngish Blue-fronted Amazon climbs to the top of its ladder. These birds are highly trainable and revel in play.

Yellow-crowned Amazon
Amazona ochrocephala (Gmelin)
1788 — 9 subspecies

1. *Amazona ochrocephala ochrocephala* (Gmelin) — Yellow-fronted Amazon

DESCRIPTION: Length approximately 36 cm.; green; cheeks, ear coverts, breast, and belly more yellowish green; forehead and lores yellow; green nape feathers with dark edging; bend of wing red; carpal edge yellow green; primaries and secondaries green, dark blue toward the tips; a red patch on the five outer feathers of the secondaries forms a speculum; underside of wing green; tail feathers green with yellow-green tips; outer tail feathers red at the base of the inner vanes; thigh yellow green, often yellowish; iris orange; orbital ring gray; bill grayish horn color; upper mandible orange gray at the base; legs gray.

Youngsters: Forehead and lores with little yellow, interspersed with many green feathers; red bend of wing less

extensive; upper mandible more grayish; iris brown.

RANGE: From northern Pará in Brazil through the Guiana states, Trinidad, Venezuela up to slopes of Andes in Norte de Santander and Meta in Colombia.

2. *Amazona ochrocephala xantholaema* Berlepsch — Marajo Amazon

DESCRIPTION: Like the nominate subspecies, but yellow on forehead more extensive; orbital ring yellowish; thigh yellow.

RANGE: Island of Marajo in the mouth of the Amazon in Brazil.

3. *Amazona ochrocephala nattereri* (Finsch) — Natterer's Amazon

DESCRIPTION: Like the nominate subspecies but somewhat larger; darker green coloration; yellow on forehead

Top: Llanos del Orinoco, Venezuela, a tree savannah with extensive cattle husbandry. *Bottom:* Blue variety of the Panama Amazon, *Amazona ochrocephala panamensis.* All of the otherwise green areas of plumage are blue in this bird.

less extensive, frequently only a small yellow patch; primaries and secondaries blue only at the tips; less red on the bend of the wing; thigh yellowish; tail feathers longer, wider yellowish green band at the tips and the red at the bases is often present only on the outer vanes.

Youngsters: Smaller yellow patch on forehead, feathers orange colored at the base; thigh yellow; iris brown.

RANGE: From western Caquetá in southern Colombia southward through eastern Ecuador to Madre de Dios in southeastern Peru, and southeastward to southwestern Amazonas in northwestern Brazil.

REMARKS: Dr. Otto Finsch named the third subspecies of the Yellow-crowned Amazon in 1864 in honor of

Panama Amazon, *Amazona ochrocephala panamensis*, with extreme extension of the yellow plumage on the forehead. Lores and stripe under the bare eye ring are also yellow.

the Austrian Johann Natterer (1781–1843): *Psittacus (Chrysotis) nattereri* Finsch 1864. Natterer spent 18 years in Brazil, Bolivia, Colombia, and Guyana, where he prepared and catalogued 12,293 birds. From these, the Zoological Institute in Vienna described 130 new species.

4. *Amazona ochrocephala panamensis* (Cabanis) — Panama Amazon

DESCRIPTION: Like the nominate subspecies, but somewhat lighter green coloration; only slight dark edging on the nape feathers; smaller yellow area on the forehead, more greenish yellow; crown bluish green; bend of wing has extensive red; thigh more yellow; bill grayish horn color with dark tip; somewhat smaller.
Youngsters: Bend of wing virtually without red coloration.
RANGE: Northwest Colombia from Magdalena south to Chocó, and

Panama including the Archipiélago de las Perlas (archipelago in the Gulf of Panama).

5. *Amazona ochrocephala auropalliata* (Lesson) — Yellow-naped Amazon

DESCRIPTION: Like the nominate subspecies, but without yellow forehead and lores (occasionally yellow feathers occur on the forehead); yellow nape band; bend of wing green; thigh green; bill grayish.
RANGE: From northwestern Nicaragua northward, along the Pacific coast to eastern Oaxaca in southern Mexico.

6. *Amazona ochrocephala parvipes* Monroe and Howell — Yellow-naped Amazon

DESCRIPTION: Like *auropalliata*, but with red on the bend of the wing; bill duller colored.

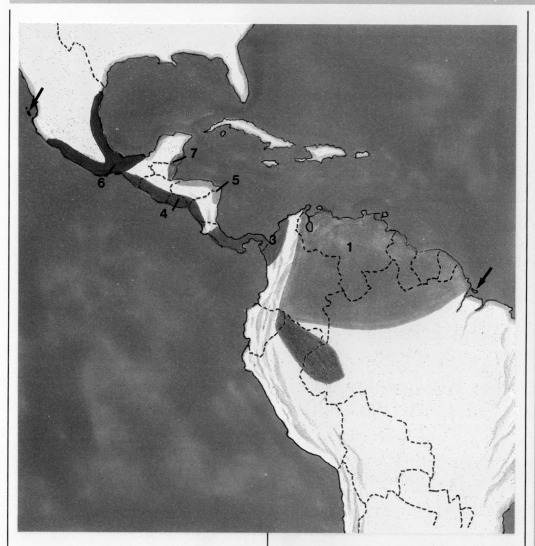

Distribution of the nine subspecies of *Amazona ochrocephala*: (1) *A. o. ochrocephala*; (2) *A. o. nattereri*; (3) *A. o. panamensis*; (4) *A. o. auropalliata*; (5) *A. o. parvipes*; (6) *A. o. oratrix*; (7) *A. o. belizensis*; (⬅ east) *A. o. xantholaema*; (⬅west) *A. o. tresmariae*.

RANGE: Along the Caribbean coast from northeastern Nicaragua to northeastern Honduras, including the Islas de la Bahía.

REMARKS: B. L. Monroe, Jr. and T. R. Howell classify the Yellow-naped Amazon occurring in the Caribbean coastal region as a separate subspecies of the Yellow-crowned Amazon.

7. *Amazona ochrocephala belizensis* Monroe and Howell

DESCRIPTION: Like *oratrix*, but darker green; yellow on the head region: forehead, lores, eye region, upper part of head, upper cheek region, and ear coverts; scattered yellow feathers on the throat and nape.

Youngsters: Yellow only on the forehead; thigh green; upper mandible brownish horn color.

RANGE: Caribbean coastal region of Belize.

REMARKS: B. L. Monroe, Jr. and T. R. Howell, who have exhaustively studied the distribution of the Yellow-crowned Amazon in Central America, classify the form occurring in Belize as a separate subspecies.

8. *Amazona ochrocephala oratrix* Ridgway — Double Yellow-headed Amazon

DESCRIPTION: Head and throat yellow; bend of wing red changing into

79

yellow; carpal edge yellow; thigh yellow; orbital ring white; bill light horn color; upper mandible somewhat darker at the base; larger and more robust.

Youngsters: Head and throat green with yellow feathers interspersed; the yellow coloration first appears in the area of the forehead and gradually spreads; bend of wing green; carpal edge yellowish green; iris brown.

RANGE: On the Caribbean and Pacific coasts of Mexico from western Campeche through Tabasco, Veracruz, southern Tamaulipas to southeastern Nuevo León and from western Chiapas through southern Oaxaca, Guerrero, and western Michoacán to Colima.

9. *Amazona ochrocephala tresmariae* Nelson — Tres Marias Amazon

DESCRIPTION: Like *oratrix*, but the yellow of the head area extends to nape and upper breast; lighter green coloration; front of body more yellowish green, suffused with light blue; bend of wing orange; median wing coverts yellow; carpal edge orange; somewhat larger.

RANGE: Islas Marías (islands off the coast of the province of Nayarit, western Mexico)

REMARKS: The nine subspecies of Amazona ochrocephala characteristically exhibit great differences in coloration within the subspecies. The Central American forms with the smallest distributions especially produce color variants that often differ significantly from the typical plumage markings.

WAY OF LIFE: Over a vast range, which stretches from the delta at the mouth of the Amazon and eastern Peru northwards as far as Mexico, nine subspecies have evolved. (Subspecies 6 and 7 have not yet been added to the *Check-List of Birds of the World*, Volume III by James Lee Peters.) The subspecies *ochrocephala*, *auropalliata*, and *oratrix* primarily inhabit the dry forests within their range, to a lesser degree rain forests, and occur at elevations of up to 700 m. The birds are not as common in coastal regions; they favor the hilly backcountry. In many areas of their range, the parrots have become followers of cultivation; that is, they readily remain along the edges of agricultural areas. The author even saw the birds in the center of the cities Port of Spain on Trinidad, Georgetown in Guyana, as well as on the outskirts of Santiago in Panama and Acapulco in Mexico. They were always very tame; one could walk under the fruit trees without their flying away. Often, the birds stayed and fed in the same trees for hours at a time. At intervals, they turned their attention to thorough preening. As a rule, the parrots departed in late afternoon in small groups, mostly in twos and threes. During flight they

Amazona ochrocephala oratrix, the Double Yellow-headed Amazon, develops its yellow coloration slowly. Youngsters possess green heads and throats—interspersed yellow feathers slowly spread downward to the neck area.

The success rate for breeding members of the species *Amazona ochrocephala* has been relatively good in the United States since the mid-1940s.

screeched energetically. When flying short distances the parrots fly just above the treetops; on longer flights, in contrast, they ascend higher. Locally, these amazons occur at variable population levels. Often areas which have been occupied for months are no longer visited after the breeding season and are avoided for a period of several months (often years).

The birds are very common in Guyana, French Guiana, northeastern Venezuela, and northern Colombia. Within its range *nattereri* is much less common. Panama Amazons are not as common as in previous years. In this case, environmental disturbance is slowly manifesting its effects. The birds are seldom seen in the Panama Canal Zone.

Wetmore (1968) reports that he observed a flock of about twenty *panamensis* on Parida Island in the Archipiélago de las Perlas (a small island chain off the Pacific coast of Panama) as they flew over to the mainland, which lies several kilometers away, in the mornings around sunrise. Wetmore suspects that the parrots go to the mainland to search for food and return to the island in the evening to roost.

The *auropalliata* amazons inhabit savanna-like scrublands. They forage along the edges of riverine forests.

Birds of the *oratrix* subspecies are found only locally in Mexico, and it appears that they are considerably more abundant on the Caribbean than on the Pacific coast. They too prefer dry deciduous forests and scrublands, but in their search for food, they also visit moist forests or the edges of rain forests.

The *tresmariae* form is relatively common on all four islands of Tres Marias. K. E. Stager (1957), on the island Maria Cleofas, the southernmost island of Tres Marias, observed a flock of approximately twenty parrots which

roosted in a stand of agave. The flock flew to its roosting site daily in the late afternoon hours. First they flew to the agave flower spikes, which can reach a height of up to eight meters. At the onset of darkness, the birds moved onto the agave leaves, where they spent the night at a height of about two meters.

The breeding season begins in northern Brazil in December and January, but is delayed until the following months in the northern parts of the range. Thus the breeding season of *oratrix* begins in May in western Mexico. In the northernmost part of their range, on the Tres Marias islands, the parrots begin incubation in February. The size of the eggs is approximately 41.8×30.9 mm. The incubation period lasts about 26 days, the nestling period of the young is about 65 days.

Yellow-naped Amazons are dwellers of the scrublands, foraging along the outer boundaries of riverine forests.

Top: Like *Amazona aestiva*, *A. ochrocephala* contains subspecies which are highly favored by the general public. The popularity of these birds is triggered by their remarkable intelligence and reliable ability to "talk."
Bottom: A Yellow-naped Amazon shelling a peanut. Besides having the ability of speech, these amazing amazons are smart, industrious, and, like their proper diet, well balanced.

CARE AND BREEDING: The subspecies *ochrocephala*, *auropalliata*, and *oratrix*, are, along with the Blue-fronted Amazon (*Amazona aestiva*), the most popular amazon parrots. The birds have a great talent for learning to talk. The author has seen many amazon parrots that could speak well and clearly, and which could at any time match Grey Parrots with respect to the range and clarity of the repeated words. The author experienced how a Yellow-naped Amazon, which was marked with a large yellow spot on the forehead in addition to the broad yellow nape band, called every afternoon to the daughter of the house playing in the garden, so that the neighbors then said, "Petra, you must go inside, your mother called." There are many episodes of this kind, and one is often amazed how appropriately particular words or even sentences are used at the right moment by the amazon parrot. The majority of imported birds are already hand-tame and able to speak a few words of Spanish.

The various subspecies of the Yellow-crowned Amazon have already been bred successfully and repeatedly in captivity. As early as 1944, *oratrix* young are said to have been raised in the United States. The Houston Zoo (USA) was able to rear three young in 1970. In 1970 in Great Britain two *oratrix* youngsters were produced, even though breeding had failed earlier in the year. In Germany, breeding apparently succeeded for the first time in 1974; two young were reared. Of the rarer *auropalliata* form, only a Swedish breeding (1974) is known. One youngster was produced, reportedly, and it left the nest box at an age of 88 (?) days. The first breeding in captivity of *panamensis* apparently took place in 1945 in the United States. In Denmark, two young in 1963 and three in 1964 were reared from a pair. The nominate form, *ochrocephala*, was successfully bred for the first time in 1967. The breeding pair was able to successfully rear additional youngsters in subsequent years. C. Smith gives the

Amazona ochrocephala oratrix begins its breeding season some time between December and May, depending on its location; in the northern parts of its range, breeding likely commences in May.

incubation period as 25 days and the nestling period as 74 days.

In Switzerland, a successful breeding of *panamensis* amazons took place in 1977. Two hand-tame, talking birds kept separately in the house were so compatible at the first attempt that their owner decided to house the birds together in a large indoor flight. A nest log of pear wood, with the dimensions 35 × 30 × 20 cm., was placed in the flight and was already visited a week later by the male. After the cock sat in the next box, he gave a peculiar call in order to lure the hen inside. Another week later the first mating attempts were observed. Thereafter, the hen also climbed inside the breeding log. A few days later the female spent the entire day inside the box and did not come out until evening. A brief inspection revealed one egg. At intervals of two days two additional eggs were laid. The female incubated without interruption and only came out of the nest for a short time daily to feed. The male kept

guard tirelessly and defended the site. After an incubation period of 28 days, a first soft peeping was detected. Two days later the next youngster hatched; the third egg was infertile (possibly the first egg laid was the infertile one, so that the incubation period was the normal 26 days). An incubation period of 25–26 days would agree with other evidence. The two youngsters developed splendidly: at 14 days they opened their eyes, in the third week they were covered in down, and a short time later the first green feathers appeared. After a nestling period of 64 days the young left the nest box. This lucky breeding shows that tame, talking amazon parrots imprinted on people are also capable of breeding, and that these animals can successfully rear their offspring.

J. Zimbal reports in *Voliere*, V:48–49, on a 1981 breeding success with the Tres Marias subspecies. Several color photographs of the youngster and the breeding pair are included in the report, from which it can be seen that the breeding pair should be classified with as the subspecies *A. o. oratrix*—this, however, in no way lessens the success. The breeding pair was housed in a roomy indoor flight with sufficient space for climbing and flying. The first mating attempts of the approximately eight-year-old pair was observed in February. One egg was laid on each of the following days: March 30, April 1, and April 3. After an incubation period of 29 (?) days, one chick hatched; the remaining two eggs were infertile. The youngster was fed well by the parents and left the next box at the age of 83 days. It is also worth mentioning that during the nestling period, the male, while the flight was cleaned as well as during the daily feeding, produced

A duo of Double Yellow-headed Amazons. Breeding pairs will naturally take to one another. It is wise, however, to ensure that your "breeding pair" consists of opposite-sex parrots. Endoscopy can provide this assurance most reliably.

loud breathing noises and feigned difficulty in breathing. This behavior has already been observed in various amazon parrot species.

The amazons kept by Leibfarth, one pair of *oratrix* birds and a mixed pair of *oratrix* and *tresmariae*, reared three chicks and one, respectively, in the summer of 1982.

The pair of blue *panamensis* kept at the zoological garden in Wasenaar, the Netherlands, were successfully bred in 1980. Two chicks were raised, which, of course, are green but heterozygous for blue.

Yellow-shouldered Amazon
Amazona barbadensis (Gmelin)
1788 — 2 subspecies

1. *Amazona barbadensis barbadensis* (Gmelin)

DESCRIPTION: Length approximately 33 cm; green; body feathers with dark edging both back and front; frontal band and lores white with isolated feathers often edged in light blue; forehead, eye region, and upper part of cheeks yellow; lower part of cheeks, ear region, and throat light bluish; occiput and nape yellow green; bend of wing yellow; carpal edge yellowish green; red speculum on four secondaries; primaries and secondaries green, on the outer vanes blue up to the tip; underside of wings blue green; thigh yellow; tail feathers green, yellowish green toward the tips; outer tail feathers red at the base, blue green on the outer vanes; iris orange, orbital ring white; bill light horn color; feet grayish.

Youngsters: Yellow head area and yellow bend of wing less extensive; iris dark brown.

RANGE: Venezuela, in the coastal regions of the provinces Falcon and (to?) Anzoategui. Last record from Aruba (island in the Dutch Antilles) is of two animals in 1955.

2. *Amazona barbadensis rothschildi* (Hartert) — Rothschild's Amazon

DESCRIPTION: Like the nominate subspecies, but bend of wing more orange colored, less extensive yellow in the head area.

RANGE: Bonaire (Dutch Antilles), as well as the islands Margarita and Blanquilla.

REMARKS: In 1892, Dr. Ernst Hartert described the second subspecies of the Yellow-shouldered

Amazona barbadensis rothschildi, Rothschild's Amazon, possesses more orange coloration on the bend of the wing than the nominate form; additionally, there is less yellow on the head.

Amazon in honor of Lord Lionel Walter Rothschild: *Chrysotis rothschild* 1892. Many other birds were named after Lord L. W. Rothschild as well.

WAY OF LIFE: Yellow-shouldered Amazons are inhabitants of dry coastal regions. On the South American continent they were observed in the coastal region of the state of Falcon and in the vicinity of the coastal city of Barcelona, Anzoategui (Phelps and Phelps 1958). On Aruba, the last authenticated observation of two birds was in 1955; since this time no further evidence of the Yellow-shouldered Amazon exists. The extirpation of the amazon parrots on the island of Aruba, as with other Caribbean island forms, can be traced to habitat destruction. In 1892, Dr. Hartert (1908, also Ferry) could report that the amazon parrots occurred in large numbers on Aruba. In 1948, only a few pairs were still recorded. In 1952, K. H. Voous reported an unsuccessful search and announced that the Yellow-shouldered Amazon had been extirpated from Aruba. The environmental disturbance on the island of Aruba is described in few words: until 1929, the island of Aruba, sterile, dry, and covered with cacti, was used for agriculture. Then the oil produced in Venezuela was brought to the island for refining, and in a few years the amounts of oil as well as the refineries grew. Today, the refineries are gigantic.

On the main island of the Dutch Antilles, Curaçao, which is affected by the petroleum industry in the same way as Aruba, amazon parrots did not occur. On Bonaire, the third and oldest island, which is quite sparsely populated (1500 inhabitants in an area of 288 square kilometers) and is only used for agriculture, a few Yellow-shouldered Amazons of the second subspecies have been able to survive till this day. Rosemary Low, a well-known

British parrot fancier, was able to visit the island of Bonaire in 1978 and published an impressive report about it in the journal *Cage and Aviary Birds*: in 1978, 400–500 amazon parrots are said to have been living on the island. A catastrophic drought hit the island and drove many of the birds into the town of Kralendijk. Some amazon parrots were shot, and many others starved. The loss was estimated at 200 individuals. The few surviving amazon parrots are spread over the entire island and wander in small groups through the arid landscape in the search for food. In the northern part of the island a former farm with an area of 2428 hectares was declared a nature preserve and now serves as a refuge for many Yellow-shouldered Amazons.

The breeding season starts in April and can last until October, depending on rainfall. Since few tree cavities are available as nest sites, the parrots use crevices and holes in cliffs as nests.

The Yellow-shouldered Amazon, the nominate *Amazona barbadensis barbadensis*, inhabits savannah-like coastal regions of Venezuela.

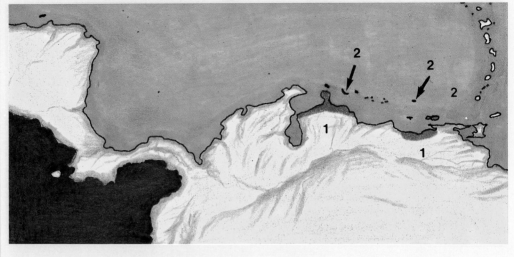

Distribution of the two subspecies of *Amazona barbadensis*: (1) *A. b. barbadensis*; (2) *A. b. rothschildi*.

Yellow-shouldered Amazon in the collection of Linda Rubin, Brookline, Massachusetts.

Two to four eggs with the dimensions 36.7 × 26.1 mm. are laid and incubated. Further particulars about the nesting habits could not be learned. The main reason for the steady decrease of the amazon-parrot population on Bonaire is the climate, namely, the rainfall that determines the food supply. The continuing expansion of the Pearly-eyed Thrasher, *Margarops fuscatus*, which occurs throughout the entire Caribbean region and as cavity nester destroys many nests, represents an additional threat to the Yellow-shouldered Amazons. Also distressing is the fact that many youngsters, even though they are completely protected on the island, are taken from the nests in order to be kept as cage birds. Many of these cage birds reach the neighboring islands of Curaçao and Aruba. In recent times, no reports of the second subspecies of the Yellow-shouldered Amazon have come from the Venezuelan islands of Blanquilla and Margarita.

CARE AND BREEDING: The nominate subspecies of the Yellow-shouldered Amazon was seldom imported. In 1979, the author was able to see a few specimens of this form at an importer's, who thought them to be juvenile *A. ochrocephala oratrix*. All eight birds were very young (dark iris) and hand-tame. They were presumably taken from the nest and raised by hand. They apparently reached Germany via Guyana.

Yellow-shouldered Amazons are reported to be very peaceable cage or aviary companions to other parrot species, and are also very compatible with much smaller species. These amazons also exhibit a considerable ability to learn noises, melodies, whistles, and words. It is a pity that the existence of these birds in their native land is so threatened, so that in the near future it will no longer be possible

Both of the subspecies of the Yellow-shouldered Amazon live in the dry coastal regions of South America. Although these birds are not common in captivity, many keepers have done quite well in rearing them.

to put these birds into the care of fanciers.

Jacobsen informed the author that in the collection of Linda Rubin, of Brookline, Massachusetts, a youngster of the subspecies *A. b. rothschildi* was bred.

At the Life Fellowship in Seffner, Florida, R. Noegel has both subspecies of the Yellow-shouldered Amazon in a breeding complex, and eggs have been laid repeatedly. Unfortunately, none had been reared successfully as of early summer, 1982, but the egg laying thus far allows one to assume that a successful breeding will soon take place, and thereby a small contribution toward the preservation of the species can be made. Both subspecies of the Yellow-shouldered Amazon are listed in Appendix I of the Washington Convention (CITES).

Amazona farinosa, the Mealy Amazon, in a natural setting. Of all the amazon species, the Mealy has the most widespread occurrence.

Mealy Amazon
Amazona farinosa (Boddaert)
1783 — 5 subspecies

1. *Amazona farinosa farinosa* (Boddaert)

DESCRIPTION: Length approximately 39 cm.; green; under parts lighter green; nape feathers have dark edging; often on the crown and forehead yellow feathers form spots, sometimes interspersed with red; on the occiput feathers green changes to violet and blue; back grayish green with a frosted effect; red speculum on the three outer secondary feathers; carpal edge red; primaries and secondaries blue toward the tips; tail feathers have a broad yellowish green tip; outer tail feathers edged with blue; iris reddish brown; orbital ring white; bill yellowish horn color; tip of upper mandible grayish; feet dark gray.

Youngsters: Iris dark brown; very few or no yellow and red feathers on the crown and forehead.

RANGE: French Guiana, Surinam, Guyana, the states of Bolívar and Amazonas in Venezuela; eastern Vaupés in Colombia. South to northwestern Bolivia and east to São Paulo in Brazil.

2. *Amazona farinosa inornata* (Salvadori) — Plain-colored Amazon

DESCRIPTION: Like the nominate subspecies, but only isolated yellow feathers on the crown and forehead.

RANGE: From northwestern Panama to extreme northwestern Venezuela and along the western side of the Andes to northwestern Ecuador; on eastern side of Andes to the Colombian department of Meta and the Venezuelan state of Amazonas.

3. *Amazona farinosa chapmani* Traylor

DESCRIPTION: Like *inornata*, but larger; lighter green; tip of tail has a broader yellowish green band.

RANGE: From the Colombian department of Vaupés southward through eastern Ecuador and eastern Peru to northwestern Bolivia.

4. *Amazona farinosa virenticeps* (Salvadori)

DESCRIPTION: Like the nominate subspecies, but somewhat lighter green overall; carpal edge yellowish green; lores and forehead bluish green; forehead green; somewhat smaller.

RANGE: From western Panama to Costa Rica and Nicaragua.

5. *Amazona farinosa guatemalae* (Sclater) — Guatemalan Amazon

DESCRIPTION: Like *virenticeps*, but blue of the head region even more extensive; somewhat larger in build.

RANGE: From Honduras along the Caribbean coast to southern Veracruz in Mexico.

WAY OF LIFE: The range of the five subspecies of the Mealy Amazon stretches from the Gulf coast in southern Veracruz in Mexico to the Atlantic coast in Espirito Santo in Brazil. Apparently they do not occur on the north side of the Orinoco in northern Venezuela and in the Brazilian states of Grande do Norte and the eastern part of Pernambuco.

The range of the Mealy Amazon is the most extensive of all the amazon-parrot species. The favorite habitat of these amazons is the tropical forest edge. They apparently avoid the unbroken, impenetrable virgin forest.

In Honduras, the form *guatemalae* occurs at elevations of up to 1200 m., where it inhabits montane rain forests. It is seldom encountered in the rain forests of the coastal regions. In Guatemala, this parrot is widely distributed in the Caribbean lowland forest as well as in the Peten region in northern Guatemala. In the Peten region, Mays found the nest of a pair of Mealy Amazons in a fissure in a stone wall of Temple IV (one of the Mayan ruins in Tikal) on April 15, 1966. Three newly hatched young were found in the crevice.

Hugh C. Land (1970) alleges that the cry of the Mealy Amazon can be heard over a distance of a mile or more.

In Belize and on the Yucatan peninsula the parrots inhabit rain forests up to an elevation of 600 m. In southern Veracruz the birds occur only

The geographic race *Amazona farinosa inornata*, whose range extends through parts of the western and eastern sides of the Andes in northwestern South America.

sporadically and appear to visit this region only to search for food. Breeding sites could not be found in Veracruz.

The fourth subspecies, *virenticeps*, inhabits landforms similar to those occupied by *guatemalae*. One often finds *virenticeps* and *inornata* birds in the company of *Amazona autumnalis salvini*. Because of the difference in size, the Mealy Amazons flying in the flock can be distinguished immediately. In Panama, except for the mountain range located in the West around the volcanic cone Chiriqui and the Serrania de Tabasara region, the birds are found throughout the entire country and also occur on the island of Coibia, located about 40 km. from the mainland. An "island race," such as is recognized with the Yellow-crowned Amazon (*Amazona ochrocephala tresmariae*) or the Orange-winged Amazon (*Amazona amazonica tobagensis*), has not evolved, however. Toward the south, the range

of *inornata* extends along the South American continent along the Pacific coast and the western slopes of the Andes as far as northwestern Ecuador. On the eastern side of the Andes, the range stretches as far as the Colombian province of Meta and in the eastern direction as far as the state of Amazonas in southwestern Venezuela. The habitat preferences of the Mealy Amazon subspecies are the same throughout their ranges. The birds are seldom encountered at elevations above 350 m. Mealy Amazons apparently do not form large flocks, as do, for example, the Orange-winged Amazons (*Amazona amazonica*). Outside the breeding season they usually accompany the other amazon-parrot and macaw species, and even with Red-vented Parrots (*Pionus menstruus*) that occur in their range. In Guatemala, the author saw them together with White-capped Parrots (*Pionus senilis*).

The daily routine of the Mealy Amazon follows the same pattern as in related species. After sunrise (in southern latitudes it becomes light very rapidly after a very short period of half-light; in the evening, night falls immediately after sunset) they stay in the vicinity of their roosting trees. About one hour later they fly in small groups to search for food. When suitable feeding trees are found, they remain in the dense crowns until the afternoon, keeping very quiet except for squabbles carried out with little noise. The return flight to the roosting sites takes place in the late afternoon, accompanied, of course, by loud screeching.

The breeding season begins approximately in December in the southern part of the range, and increasingly later in the northern areas (as late as the beginning of April in Mexico). As a rule, three eggs are laid and incubated. According to Schönwetter (1964), the elliptical eggs

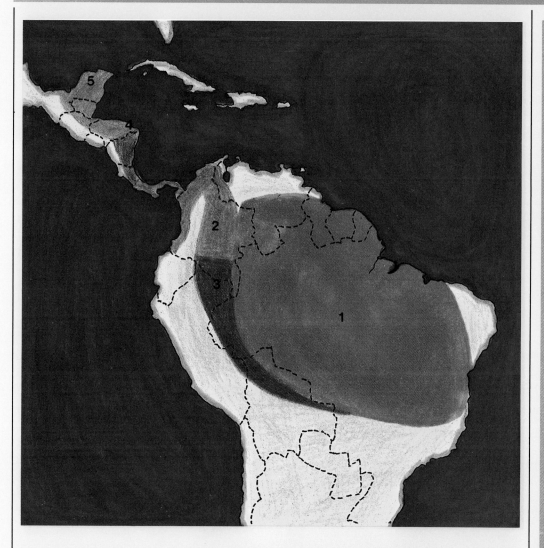

have dimensions of about 37.7 × 29.0 mm. There is no data concerning the length of incubation and the nestling period. As with other amazon-parrot species, the incubation period is probably 25–26 days. The nestling period of the young doubtless lasts at least three months.

CARE AND BREEDING: Karl Neunzig (1920) already reported that the Mealy Amazon was easy to tame and teach and could learn to talk well. As a tame bird, this one was also a dreadful screecher. The author has kept several Mealy Amazons (*A. f. farinosa* and *A. f. guatemalae*), and had concluded that the birds were always quiet. Even the other amazon parrots kept in neighboring flights, raising their voices in the morning and evening hours, could not stimulate the Mealy Amazons to join in. It seemed, except for a few growling sounds, almost as if they were mute. Only a hand-tame bird placed in my care, which spent about three weeks of its "vacation" in the aviary complex, demonstrated what loud screeching these birds are capable of. To be sure, the Mealy Amazon placed in my care only screeched twice for about five minutes at a time. But in volume of sound, it can be compared with the large cockatoos.

Mealy Amazons are seldom offered for sale. Because of their quiet nature and the deliberate behavior, they are

Top: The Mealy Amazon, *Amazona farinosa farinosa*, has a good reputation for peaceful cohabitation with other parrots. *Bottom:* The Guatemalan Amazon, *Amazona farinosa guatemalae.* Note the distinct difference between the upper-head coloration of these two conspecifics.

highly recommended as cage and aviary birds. Without reservation, one can keep them together with other parrots, even smaller species. It appears that Mealy Amazons go out of their way to avoid a fight. When excited, they fan out their nape feathers and produce growling sounds.

The Mealy Amazons kept by the author ate half-ripe corn in unbelievable quantities. Each bird devoured up to three ears a day. They also took beechnuts, cembra-pine nuts, hazelnuts, and all kinds of fruit very readily. With fruits such as cherries and plums, their main interest was the pit; the flesh was usually torn off so as to obtain the pit as quickly as possible.

In both 1980 and 1981, in the aviaries of A. E. Decoteau, two youngsters of the subspecies *A. f. farinosa* were produced. In the breeding register of the British Parrot Society of 1978, a captive breeding of the subspecies *A. f. inornata* with two young reared is reported.

In the author's experiences, the Mealy Amazon, *Amazona farinosa farinosa*, demonstrates great fondness for half-ripe corn. Additionally, it was found that this parrot's main interest was in the pit and not the flesh of fruits.

Artist's rendering of *Amazona mercenaria mercenaria*, the Scaly-naped Amazon, also known as the Mercenary Amazon. The author considers *A. m. mercenaria* as well as *A. m. canipalliata* to be geographic races of *A. farinosa*.

Scaly-naped Amazon
Amazona mercenaria (Tschudi)
1844 — 2 subspecies

1. *Amazona mercenaria mercenaria* (Tschudi) — Mercenary Amazon

DESCRIPTION: Length approximately 34 cm.; green; forehead and under parts lighter green; upper part of head, nape, and cheeks grayish green with dark edging; upper back and sides of cheeks dark green with dark edging; carpal edge yellow to orange; primaries and secondaries green, blue toward tips; red speculum on the three outer secondaries; underside of wing green; tail feathers green, yellow green at the tips; outer tail feathers green at the base, followed by a dark red spot, then yellow green toward tips; iris orange; orbital ring grayish white; bill grayish, horn colored at the base; feet grayish brown.

Youngsters: Brown iris, supposedly.

RANGE: Along the eastern slope of the Andes from northwestern Bolivia to northern Peru.

2. *Amazona mercenaria canipalliata* (Cabanis)

DESCRIPTION: Like the nominate subspecies, but speculum on the three outer secondaries reddish brown.

RANGE: Eastern Ecuador on the eastern slopes of the Western Cordillera and on the western slopes of the Eastern Cordillera; Colombia from south to north along the eastern slopes of the Central Cordillera and on the western slopes of the Eastern Cordillera; northwestern Venezuela on the southern western slopes of the Cordillera de Merida.

REMARKS: *Amazona mercenaria* is a typical example of the taxonomic treatment of the species and subspecies in the genus *Amazona*. Unfortunately, there are only very few museum specimens of this "species." Detailed observations in the wild regarding the social, nesting, and breeding behavior are also lacking; nevertheless the author considers the two subspecies of *Amazona mercenaria* to be geographic races of *Amazona farinosa*. Two points speak in favor of this thesis: firstly, the virtually identical plumage coloration of both "species," and, secondly, the area inhabited by *Amazona m. mercenaria* and *A. m. canipalliata*, with almost no gaps, adjoins the ranges of *Amazona farinosa inornata* and *A. f. chapmani*, essentially without overlap.

WAY OF LIFE: Scaly-naped Amazons are birds of temperate climatic zones and inhabit elevations up to 3500 m. in extremely inaccessible regions. From the very few observations that have been made in the wild, one must assume that these amazon parrots occur only in small numbers throughout their range. It is noteworthy that the birds seek out the higher mountain regions, in which the nights are noticeably cool, for roosting. In the morning the Scaly-naped Amazons fly back to the forested valleys to search for food. Ramirez, a great naturalist, informed the author in 1977 that inhabitants of the western slopes of the Pico Bolivar (5007 m.), in the vicinity of Merida, northwestern Venezuela, observed a flock of about 60 Scaly-naped Amazons in the forested areas at an elevation of approximately 2800 m. Ramirez later searched for these rare birds in the reported area for days but found no sign of them. Apparently the birds were migrating and stopped on the forested mountain slopes for only a short time. Although Ramirez lived in the Cordillera de Merida for many years, he was never granted the opportunity to observe Scaly-naped Amazons in the wild. Probably the animals occur only locally in northwestern Venezuela in

Distribution of the two *Amazona mercenaria* subspecies: (1) *A. m. canipalliata*; (2) *A. m. mercenaria*.

exceedingly small numbers, so that in many regions they are found seldom or not at all. On the western slopes of the East Cordillera in Cundinamarca, Colombia, they could no longer be located, despite an intensive search. In northern Colombia, as well as in Ecuador, eastern Peru, and northwestern Bolivia, the birds are also rare, if somewhat more common than in the northernmost part of their range.

CARE AND BREEDING: The Scaly-naped Amazon, which gives the impression of a smaller version of the Mealy Amazon (*Amazona farinosa*), is probably not in the possession of European bird fanciers (?); at least no birds are recognized as this "species." In 1981 and 1982, several shipments of parrots reached Germany from Ecuador. It would have by no means been surprising had some of the Mealy Amazons imported from this region turned out to be Scaly-naped Amazons. It is certain that the London Zoo had a Scaly-naped Amazon. No other substantiated reports of captive birds exist, which is by no means surprising, in view of the circumstances cited above.

Lilac-crowned Amazon
Amazona finschi (Sclater) 1864 — 2
subspecies

1. *Amazona finschi finschi* (Sclater)

DESCRIPTION: Length approximately
32 cm; green, under parts lighter,
feathers edged; lores and forehead dark
red; crown of head and sides of nape
greenish blue; cheeks yellowish green
up to ear region, merging into blue;
narrow, dark-blue stripe behind eye;
primaries green, violet blue toward
tips; red spots on the outer vanes of the
outer five secondaries form a
speculum; secondaries green, blue
toward tips; underside of wing green;
tail feathers green, more yellowish
green toward tips; iris orange; orbital
ring gray; bill yellowish; feet grayish.
Youngsters: Colors duller; iris
brown.
RANGE: Western Mexico from
Durango and Sinaloa southward to
Oaxaca.

2. *Amazona finschi woodi* Moore

DESCRIPTION: Like the nominate
subspecies, but somewhat darker; red
on forehead somewhat restricted;
length about 33 cm.
RANGE: Northwestern Mexico from
central Durango and central Sinaloa
northward to southeastern Sonora and
southwestern Chihuahua.

REMARKS: In 1864, after the British
Museum obtained a beautiful specimen
of the Lilac-crowned Amazon prepared
by Dr. Otto Finsch, Dr. P. L. Sclater
put forward a motion to name this
amazon parrot after Dr. Otto Finsch:
Chrysotis finschi. Prof. Dr. Friedrich
Hermann Otto Finsch (October 8,
1839–January 31, 1917) was an eminent
ethnologist, as well as a respected
ornithologist and the author of

significant books. Particularly
noteworthy is his book *Die Papageien*
('The Parrots'), 1867–1868.
The Latin name is often written with
ii at the end, for example, *Micropsitta
finschii finschii* (Finsch's Pygmy-
Parrot).
The other subspecies of the Lilac-
crowned Amazon, *Amazona finschi
woodi*, was named in 1937 by Robert T.
Moore after Dr. Casey A. Wood, in
recognition of his ornithological work.
WAY OF LIFE: Mexico, with its
varied landforms and vegetation zones,
still provides both subspecies of the
Lilac-crowned Amazon with a largely
untouched environment. In 1976, the
author made an extensive trip in
Mexico, which included the range of
the Lilac-crowned Amazon. The visit
took place during the months of April
to June, and thus was relatively
unfavorable for close observations of
parrots: since the breeding season of
the Lilac-crowned Amazon occurs
during this period, the animals are not

The Sierra Madre
Occidental,
Mexico, a hot arid
upland zone with a
semi-desert–like
character.

in flocks and therefore are not as conspicuous. The breeding season of the nominate subspecies begins in February or March. The other subspecies, found farther to the north, does not begin breeding until about May. In the region between Taxco and Chilpancingo in the state of Guerrero, in the late afternoon hours, small flocks of two to six Lilac-crowned Amazons were observed several times with

Lilac-crowned Amazon, *Amazona finschi finschi*, **also called Finsch's Amazon. The breeding season of this amazon occurs from April to June, during which time the birds do not form flocks but exist in pairs.**

binoculars in an inaccessible area. The region in which the birds stayed was about 1000 m. above sea level and was interspersed with small stands of trees as well as cacti. The birds allowed an approach to within 100 m., but then flew away with loud cries. About 40 km. northwest of Guadalajara, in the state of Jalisco, a region reminiscent of Central European deciduous forests in appearance and vegetation, pairs of Lilac-crowned Amazons in flight were observed repeatedly. In the treetops of

large oaks, which they preferred, they could not be discerned. Lilac-crowned Amazons were rather well represented in this region; at the same time, a few White-fronted Amazons (*Amazona albifrons saltuensis*), which only flew about in pairs, were observed.

On the outskirts of Guadalajara, the author met a bird dealer on his way to town. One of the three trunks he was carrying contained song birds, in the two others were amazon parrots. One trunk with a floor of about 80 × 60 cm. and a height of about 20 cm. was occupied by approximately 50 (!) amazon parrots. A few of the birds had rich, brilliant yellow head plumage and an intense orangish red bend of the wing; the remaining coloration was identical to that of the Lilac-crowned Amazon. A specific determination could not be made; to be sure, there was a certain similarity to *Amazona ochrocephala oratrix*, but the particular parts of the plumage gave rise to considerable doubt. Because of language difficulties, the dealer could not be questioned. The only thing that could be learned was that the birds were either captured or taken from the nests about 100 km. north of Guadalajara. On the spot, two animals, one Lilac-crowned Amazon as well as one unidentifiable amazon parrot, were purchased from the dealer. Two cages and food were obtained promptly, and the birds were nicely accommodated in the motor home. The two birds survived the entire Mexican trip of over 10,000 km. as well as the flight to Germany very well. The species or subspecies to which the peculiarly colored amazon belonged could not be determined in Germany either. It was suspected that it might be a hybrid of *finschi* and *ochrocephala oratrix*. We finally learned the answer in the following year, once it molted: it "developed" into an exquisite Lilac-crowned Amazon. Apparently, in its

Amazona finschi finschi, the Lilac-crowned Amazon. Note the red forehead and yellowish green cheeks characteristic of this race.

The Lilac-crowned Amazon, *Amazona finschi finschi*, inhabits western Mexico, with a range from Durango and Sinaloa southward to Oaxaca. The varied terrain and vegetation of this region afford this parrot a relatively safe harbor.

homeland the bird had been fed some substance that induced the yellow coloration.

Throughout their range along the Pacific coast, Lilac-crowned Amazons are a relatively common parrot. The animals appear to stay in the tropical coastal regions only in the winter months; at other times they occupy the forested slopes of the Sierra Madre Occidental up to elevations of 2200 m. J. M. Forshaw (1965) reported a sighting of a rather small number of this parrot species inland from San Blas, Nayarit. W. J. Schaldach, Jr. (1963) frequently saw the birds in Colima, where they were encountered both at sea level and in the temperate-zone oak woodlands. In Colima, Schaldach was able to observe in February a pair of Lilac-crowned Amazons that showed an interest in an old woodpecker hole in a dead gum tree which stood in a high, tropical deciduous forest. L. C. Binford (1968)

suggests that the birds are rare inhabitants of the moist and semi-arid forests and are found at elevations up to 1500 m. in the Pacific region in Oaxaca. In the fall, the birds wander as far as the Isthmus of Tehuantepec.

The communal search for food that takes place outside the breeding season is done in small groups. The amazon parrots invade corn fields very readily and do considerable damage to the crop. In the late afternoon the birds assemble in their roosting trees once more. In such groups of trees, one often sees 200–300 amazons, making a racket into the late evening hours.

CARE AND BREEDING: Lilac-crowned Amazons, the nominate subspecies for the most part, have recently been available more frequently in the animal trade. These appealingly colored birds are quite lively and also like to fly, which cannot be said of many of the related species. When furnishing an aviary for this parrot species, one should make very certain that the birds have sufficient room to fly. The author has kept Lilac-crowned Amazons for several years and has observed quite different traits and behaviors among them. On one occasion in November, a hand-tame bird escaped. Ten days passed before the amazon parrot was found, about two km. from the house. A farmer who was able to observe it during this time said that the Lilac-crowned Amazon had perched in a tall poplar right beside a four-lane highway. From this tree, an unharvested corn field, about two hundred meters away, was visited twice a day, in the morning from about eight to ten o'clock and in the afternoon from three to five o'clock. First the bird flew to an apple tree standing beside the field, and then, after it had made sure there was no danger, it flew into the corn field. In the brief period of liberty, the amazon had become wild again, and only allowed the author to

approach to a distance of three meters before flying back to the tall poplar. After not succeeding in capturing the Lilac-crowned Amazon for two days, a parrot cage, the sort common in the trade and from which the floor had been removed and replaced with a large grille, was placed in the apple tree. A string about 30 m. long was tied to the opened grille. Treats placed inside the cage were supposed lure the amazon parrot into the cage. The next morning the temperature was about 2°C, and the amazon parrot was perched inside the cage, so that the string had only to be pulled for the grille to snap shut. At home the amazon parrot immediately flew onto the hand and was not

otherwise shy either. Despite the low temperatures at night, the bird had survived the twelve days of freedom very well.

Another male Lilac-crowned Amazon in the author's possession struck up a close friendship with a female Yellow-headed Amazon (*Amazona ochrocephala oratrix*), which has been a vacation guest twice a year. The greeting takes place with a great fuss; moreover, the pupils are strongly contracted so that the orange-colored iris stands out brilliantly, the wings are extended, and the nape feathers are ruffled. The greeting ceremony lasts almost a full hour. They spend the time after that courting, fighting, and

Pair of Lilac-crowned Amazons, *Amazona finschi finschi*, outside their nestbox. Most breeders recommend offering a pair several nextboxes to allow the birds free choice of a breeding site.

playing with each other. Other Yellow-headed Amazons are ignored by this Lilac-crowned Amazon.

In the San Diego Zoo, breeding was successful in 1951. After an incubation period of 28 (?) days, one youngster hatched and was reared from the fifth day onwards by hand. The bird ate on its own for the first time at the age of three months; four weeks later it was totally self-sufficient.

The first successful European breeding of the Lilac-crowned Amazon took place in 1978 in England (Mann 1978). The two Lilac-crowned Amazons were purchased in 1974. Both birds were placed in an indoor flight connected to another outdoors. When the birds were closely compared, one could notice that one had a somewhat larger build and a more massive head. The birds got on well with each other, and they were thought to be a pair. At first the owner had misgivings about placing the birds in the outdoor flight, because their cries were expected to create a disturbance. These misgivings were soon dispelled, however, since both birds behaved very quietly, and in no time at all won the friendship of the neighbors, who enjoyed the birds' animated activity. The parrots took an

interest in a tree trunk placed in the flight only until it had been gnawed to pieces. Later a smaller nest box was installed.

The first courtship display was observed in May of 1978. The hen screeched and thereby attracted the cock. Inspired by the hen's behavior, he adopted the drooping-wing posture and courted. Afterwards, the hen was regularly fed by the cock. Soon the first matings took place; this was always accomplished from the cock's right side and the hen's left side. Toward the end, the cock always stretched out his wings completely. During copulation, both birds produced soft humming sounds. When mating was finished, the birds disappeared into the nest box for a long time. During the nest inspection carried out on the 2nd of June, one egg was found in the hollow, which was lined with wood shavings. The second egg must have been laid a few days later. The female sat very tightly and only left the nest box for several minutes in early evening. An inspection carried out on the 28th of June revealed that one egg was fertile. On the 3rd of July, the hen came out of the nest already in the morning. Upon immediate inspection a chick with a sparse covering of down was discovered (the second egg was infertile). The youngster was cared for by the parents very well, so that it grew quickly. It opened its eyes on the 15th day of life. The youngster was already ninety percent feathered on the 12th of August, so that the red forehead and the lilac-colored crown were already distinguishable. At this time, the youngster was very venturesome and often showed itself at the entrance hole of the nest box. As soon as it felt it was being watched, it hissed softly. When picked up, it was exceedingly tame. On the 29th of August, at an age of about 60 days, the youngster left the nest box. It was somewhat slighter in stature than the adult birds. The red feathers on the forehead were more extensive but, in comparison to the adults, the lilac coloration of the crown was limited. The iris was dark brown. The youngster initially had difficulty flying and often fell. It was captured every evening and placed in the nest box. On the 16th of December, after it was completely independent, it was brought inside the house.

During rearing, the following foods were offered: peanuts, sunflower seeds, hemp seeds, nuts, apples, oranges, and bread soaked in fruit nectar.

In Canada, this species was bred for the first time in 1972. The breeding pair reared three young for R. E. McPeek. In the United States, broods are successfully reared every year, and it is particularly encouraging that fanciers do not cross the subspecies *A. f. finschi* with *A. f. woodi* but instead in breeding attempts strive to pair individuals of the same subspecies.

According to data from Schönwetter (1964), the dimensions of the eggs are 37.0 × 29.2 mm.

Amazona finschi finschi perched attentively on a natural tree branch. During incubation, the male will often keep watchful guard over the nest while the female warms the eggs.

Below: Pair of free-flying Green-cheeked Amazons, *Amazona viridigenalis,* positioned on a tree in Florida. Green-cheeked Amazons occur in a wide variety of habitats, and many specimens have adjusted well to outdoor keeping in the Florida environment. *Opposite:* Green-cheeked Amazon, *Amazona viridigenalis,* displaying the bright red forehead and lores characteristic of the species.

Green-cheeked Amazon
Amazona viridigenalis (Cassin) 1853

DESCRIPTION: Length approximately 33 cm.; green, dark edging; breast and belly lighter green; forehead, lores, upper part of head bright red; occiput to nape greenish blue; blue band beginning over the eye and extending to the side of the neck, bounded by cheeks and ear region; cheeks green, no edging; speculum red; outer vanes of the primaries blue, green toward base; secondaries green, blue toward base; tail green, yellowish green toward tip; iris orange; orbital ring gray; bill yellowish; feet grayish.

Female: Red on upper part of head less extensive.

Youngsters: Only forehead and lores red.

RANGE: Northeastern Mexico in eastern Nuevo Léon, Tamaulipas, eastern San Luis Potosi, eastern Hidalgo and northern Veracruz.

WAY OF LIFE: The range of the Green-cheeked Amazon, in northeastern Mexico, on the eastern side of the Madre Oriental as far as the Gulf of Mexico, is relatively small but nevertheless consists of extremely varied habitats. The mountain regions are bordered by narrow coastal plains on the Gulf of Mexico. In the north, the Rio Bravo forms the boundary of the range. Although the landform continues unchanged across the border into the United States, no parrot species is found there (with the exception of the Thick-billed Parrot, *Rhynchopsitta pachyrhyncha pachyrhyncha,* which wanders as far as the mountains of southern Arizona). Green-cheeked Amazons occur in very diverse habitats. In Veracruz, the birds favor the low-lying tropical rain forests. In southern Tamaulipas the animals prefer the little montane forests, consisting primarily of oak (*Quercus*) and pine (*Pinus*) species, found in the river valleys of the subtropical and temperate zones. The seeds of these trees are very readily eaten. Green-cheeked Amazons often invade corn fields. Corn is the most important dietary staple in Mexico, so amazons and other parrots that invade corn fields are ruthlessly shot and chased away.

The breeding season starts at the beginning of April. Like all amazon parrots, Green-cheeked Amazons use tree cavities or old woodpecker holes. As a rule, three to five eggs, about 35.7 × 27.5 mm., are laid and incubated. No data exist concerning the length of the incubation and nestling periods. After the young are reared and are self-sufficient, the families again assemble

into small groups, including Red-lored Amazons (*Amazona autumnalis autumnalis*) and Yellow-headed Amazons (*Amazona ochrocephala oratrix*) as well, in order to search for food together. G. H. Lowery, Jr. and W. W. Dalquest (*Birds from the state of Veracruz, Mexico*, 1951) indicate that

Green-cheeked Amazons are practically never found on the slopes of the Mexican plateau and could be sighted only a few times in the coastal plain of central Veracruz. They are more common in northern Veracruz as well as in the other states of the north. The Ornate Hawk-Eagle, *Spizaetus ornatus*,

Amazona viridigenalis sitting candidly and colorfully on its natural perch. The Green-cheeked Amazon is a relatively common aviary and cage inhabitant in the United States.

which has become specialized to hunting parrots in a portion of its range, includes Green-cheeked Amazons among its prey.

CARE AND BREEDING: In the United States one sees Green-cheeked Amazons in the fanciers' aviaries quite often. They are kept singly as cage birds just as frequently. The first authenticated importation of Green-cheeked Amazons to Germany took place in 1878, and they have been imported sporadically ever since. Usually it is young birds, for the most part recognizable by the small amount of red on the forehead, that are available.

The author, having taken care of six individuals of this species in 1978 and 1979, can testify that Green-cheeked Amazons are very lively and raise their shrill voices very loudly, particularly in the morning and evening hours. All six birds were about 18 to 24 months old and became fully colored after the two years of age. They fed on beechnuts, acorns, and the seeds from pine and fir cones with relish. When playing with members of their own species, and also when excited, the birds erected their nape feathers like a fan. The contraction of the pupils in the Green-cheeked Amazon is extreme, to pin-head size, and the orange-colored iris stands out brilliantly. "Play with the eyes" becomes a real spectacle in the

Headstudy of one-year-old Green-cheeked Amazon, *Amazona viridigenalis*. The characteristic orange iris and the beginning of a blue band forming above the rear of the eye are clearly visible.

context of spreading the tail feathers and extending the wing feathers accompanied by piercing cries. The "band of six" did not tolerate other amazon-parrot species. The Blue-headed Parrots, *Pionus menstruus menstruus*, kept in the adjoining flight were immediately attacked and bitten on the feet as soon as they hung on the bars between the flights.

J. Mattmann, a Swiss fancier, has had two Green-cheeked Amazons for over five years. When the birds were purchased, it could not be determined whether they were a pair. Two years later it was noticed that the head of one of the birds had become more massive, so it was suspected that they were a pair. The first eggs were laid in July of 1979, but it soon became evident that they were infertile. A year later (the birds were kept in an outdoor flight with dimensions of 3.5 × 2.0 × 2.0 m.

and a connecting indoor flight of about 1 cubic meter) they again exhibited mutual interest. Shortly thereafter the first copulations were observed. The two birds became increasingly aggressive toward their keeper and also reacted very nervously to disturbances. The first egg was found on the 14th of July; a second was discovered three days later. The female incubated continuously from this time on. The male kept guard the entire time and proved very aggressive. The first peeping one of the chicks was heard on the 12th of August. Thus the incubation period amounted to 26 days. From this point on, infant fruit muesli mixed with rearing food was added to the very wide assortment of foods offered. Both parents fed the youngsters equally well and were solicitous. In the first six weeks of life the little amazons were extremely quiet. On the 20th of October they were observed outside the nest box for the first time; they also busied themselves at the food bowl. The nestling period therefore lasted from the 12th of August to the 20th of October, an interval of 69 days. At the age of four months, the young looked almost identical to the adults; only the smaller bill size and the smaller amount of red on the head still identified them as young birds.

In 1934, a cross-breeding with the much smaller White-fronted Amazon (*Amazona albifrons*) succeeded in England.

In the aviaries of B. Boswell, Natal, South Africa, a youngster was bred in 1976 (*Avic. Mag.*, 83:214).

According to the breeding register of the England's Parrot Society, J. Stoodley succeeded in rearing five Green-cheeked Amazons in 1979. The American fancier L. Brandt had the same success in 1981. Here too, five young were reared.

Considering the popularity of the Green-cheeked Amazon, there are likely a number of very successful breeding programs about which the author is not familiar.

Top: Fortunately for the parrot fancy, breeders have enjoyed good success with breeding and rearing the Green-cheeked Amazon, *Amazona viridigenalis*. *Bottom:* Green-cheeked Amazon spreading its wings for an afternoon stretch in the aviary.

Red-lored Amazon, *Amazona autumnalis autumnalis*, casting a rather cynical glance from its favorite outpost. Some fanciers consider the yellow, red, and blue facial markings of this parrot to be among the most attractive in the amazon parrot world.

Red-lored Amazon
Amazona autumnalis (Linnaeus)
1758 — 3 subspecies

1. *Amazona autumnalis autumnalis* (Linnaeus)

DESCRIPTION: Length 34 cm.; green (under parts yellowish green); forehead and lores red; crown blue; occiput and nape green changing into lilac blue, black edging; yellow below the eye and on the forward cheek region, feathers partially red at the base; carpal edge yellowish green; red speculum on five of the secondaries; secondaries green, dark blue toward tips; primaries green, blue at tips; underside of wing light green; tail feathers green, toward tips yellowish green; iris orange; orbital ring white; upper mandible horn colored, grayish at the tip; lower mandible grayish horn color; feet grayish.

Youngsters: Forehead and lores less red; green feathers interspersed in yellow cheek region; iris dark brown.

RANGE: Along the Caribbean coast from Tamaulipas in northeastern Mexico southward to northeastern Nicaragua as well as on the islands Roatán and Barbareta (Islas de la Bahía) off the eastern coast of Honduras.

2. *Amazona autumnalis salvini* (Salvadori) — Salvin's Amazon

DESCRIPTION: Like the nominate subspecies, but darker green; red on forehead less extensive; cheeks greenish yellow; ear region blackish green; outer tail feathers red at the base of the inner vanes, on the outer vanes blue.

Youngsters: Forehead and lores less red; iris dark brown.

RANGE: From southeastern Nicaragua through eastern and southwestern Costa Rica and Panama to extreme northwestern Venezuela (along the Caribbean coast) and southward to southwestern Colombia (along the Pacific coast).

REMARKS: The second subspecies of the Red-lored Amazon was named by the famous Italian ornithologist Conte Adelardo Tommasco Salvadori Paleotti (1835–1923) in honor of the English ornithologist Osbert Salvin (1835–1881): *Chrysotis salvini* (1891).

This Red-lored Amazon, *Amazona autumnalis autumnalis*, communicates avidly with approaching visitors. Without fear, these amazons prefer the outer edge of the rain forest, from where they can easily raid farmers' plantations and fields.

3. *Amazona autumnalis lilacina*
Lesson — Lilacine Amazon

DESCRIPTION: Like *salvini*, but more olive green; forehead and lores red; crown to occiput reddish lilac; forward cheek region yellowish; ear region greenish yellow; chin and throat light green, pink at the bases; primaries and secondaries green; primaries blue at the tips, gray on the inner vanes; sixth and seventh secondaries red on the central portion of the outer vane; bill brownish black.

Youngsters: Coloration on the head noticeably paler; crown and occiput greenish; cheeks more greenish yellow; iris brown.

RANGE: Along the Pacific coast in western Ecuador southward to the Gulf of Guayaquil and northward to the Colombian border.

REMARKS: The author has treated the fourth subspecies (*Amazona autumnalis diadema*) as a separate species.

WAY OF LIFE: The three subspecies of the Red-lored Amazon occur in the tropical zones of their range. As a rule, they inhabit lowlands up to an elevation of 350 m. In Veracruz, Mexico, Red-lored Amazons occur at elevations of up to approximately 625 m. In Honduras, these birds are found up to an elevation of 1100 m. Outside the breeding season, as many as a thousand amazon parrots assemble at their ancestral roosting trees, and then fly off the next morning in pairs or in small groups in search of food. The birds favor the edges of the rain forests, from which they can invade fruit plantations and corn fields. In northeastern Mexico, in Tamaulipas, one finds these amazon parrots relatively often in moist lowlands.

In Veracruz, Mexico, the birds are very abundant throughout the entire state. Loetscher states that, except for the Aztec Conure, *Aratinga astec astec*, these amazon parrots are the most widely distributed parrot species in southern Veracruz. In the Mexican states of eastern San Luis Potosi, eastern Puebla, eastern Oaxaca, Tabasco, northern Chiapas, and southern Campeche, the birds live along the river courses; however, they are not as abundant in this region. In Quintana Roo (Yucatan peninsula), the amazons seem to be present only outside the breeding season. For Yucatan, no incidence could be substantiated. Red-lored Amazons are found in great numbers in Belize, northeastern and eastern Guatemala, northern and eastern Honduras, and northeastern Nicaragua. The amazon parrots could no longer be sighted on Utila in 1963 (Monroe), although they were found there in large numbers in 1937 (Bond). By comparison, on the islands of Roatán and Barbareta, which also belong to the Islas de la Bahía, they are numerous in the forests.

Salvin's Amazon, the second subspecies of the Red-lored Amazon, inhabits the same environments as the nominate form and is just as common through its range. In the lowlands of Panama, in the tropical forests and on the edges of forests, and on the islands Coiba, Escudo de Veraguas, and the

Archipiélago de las Perlas, small groups of these birds in flight are sighted regularly. One can barely detect the birds while feeding and during the midday rest period, since they are very quiet at these times. If one disturbs them, they fly off with a great outcry. The author was able to startle Salvin's Amazons a number of times in Panama, and each time was astonished at the unbelievable racket the birds produced in flight. For a fairly long period of time, the author was able to observe a Salvin's Amazon family, two adults with three young, in the vicinity of La Chorrera, just outside the Panama Canal Zone. The animals were perched in the top of an approximately 20 m. high palm and fed heartily on the nut-size palm fruits. The youngsters could be very easily distinguished from the parents by their clumsy behavior. As a bird of prey suddenly circled at a distance of about 500 m., the five amazons flew away in a panic with loud cries. During flight the slowly beating wings do not extend above rump level. Amazon parrots can be recognized immediately by their characteristic flight style. Red-lored Amazons, rare in northeastern and northwestern Colombia as well as in extreme northwestern Venezuela, can be found only sporadically in the lowland tropical rain forests. The amazon parrots again become more common in the Pacific area in southwestern Colombia.

The breeding season of the three subspecies of the Red-lored Amazon begins in October in the southern portion of their range, in Ecuador and southwest Colombia, and shifts into the following months as one proceeds northward. In Tamaulipas, northwestern Mexico, in the northernmost part of the range, they do not begin breeding until April. Two to four eggs, with a size of approximately 39.2 × 30.5 mm., are

Pair of Lilacine Amazons, *Amazona autumnalis lilacina*. This amazon race was particularly abundant in Veracruz, Mexico, when visited by Loetscher. Outside the breeding season, as many as one thousand parrots may convene at a roosting site.

laid and incubated for about 25 days in tree cavities and abandoned woodpecker nests. There is no data concerning the nestling period.

CARE AND BREEDING: Small numbers of all three subspecies have been imported and offered by the animal trade time and again in recent years. The very attractively colored nominate subspecies with the brilliant yellow cheeks is the most common. During the acclimation period one must make sure that the birds are kept in warm accommodations and that the nighttime temperature does not fall below 18°C. After acclimation, the birds are quite hardy and can be kept in the garden or on the balcony throughout the summer months.

The American H. Prenner has kept Red-lored Amazons with great success. Prenner's interest is concentrated on this species, and so he keeps several pairs in his aviaries. The first breeding attempts ended without success. A small wine cask with a diameter of about 35 cm. served as a nest site; a layer of peat was placed on the bottom; on top of that was a layer of sawdust approximately 5 cm. thick. Three fertile eggs were laid in the third breeding attempt, and three young hatched at the end of the incubation period and were then reared by adults. Over the course of many years, Prenner's Red-lored Amazons have

Top: Sideview of the Red-lored Amazon, *Amazona autumnalis autumnalis.* The author reports that there are no known German breeding successes with this or the other two races of the *A. autumnalis* species. *Bottom:* Frontview of *Amazona autumnalis autumnalis,* in which the blue coloration of the head is clearly visible. *Opposite:* An *A. autumnalis* specimen. Until recently, the Diademed Amazon, *A. diadema,* was considered a race of the *A. autumnalis* species.

(*Parkieten Soc.*, 14:24).

In 1956, the English fancier E. N. T. Vane (*Avic. Mag.*, 63:73–188) succeeded in rearing a young Red-lored Amazon with the aid of a Grey Parrot, *Psittacus erithacus.* After the amazon-parrot pair attempted to breed for several years without success, in 1956 the eggs were placed under a tame, singly kept female Grey Parrot that had laid eggs annually. One youngster hatched after an incubation period of approximately 25–26 days. The foster mother raised the little amazon parrot with the greatest care. After about ten days of age, the amazon parrot opened its eyes; after four weeks the first feather sheaths emerged. At an age of seven weeks the youngster is said to have looked like the adults already, and after the eighth week it was almost self-sufficient.

raised more than twenty young.

Salvin's Amazon, which like the nominate form is very lively and noisy, seldom reaches the hands of bird fanciers. No German breeding successes are known for this form, nor for *A. a. autumnalis* and *A. a. lilacina.* In 1979, two Salvin's Amazons were reared by the Dutchman R. v. Dieten (*Parkieten Soc.*, 14:24). Three young were bred by the English fancier D. Spilsbury in 1980 (*Avic. Mag.*, 87:148).

The subspecies *A. a. lilacina*, which differs markedly in coloration from the two previously mentioned subspecies, has been imported more frequently in recent years. The author saw several singly kept specimens that were extremely tame and confiding. Among them was one that with great pleasure allowed itself to be laid on its back and have its belly stroked. This bird was cared for by a retired couple, who occupied themselves with the bird the whole day.

Two *lilacina* young are said to have been reared in the United States as early as 1946. Jacobsen communicates that this success occurred in the aviaries of Putman.

In 1980, the Dutchman R. v. Dieten obtained two youngsters from a breeding pair of Lilacine Amazons

Diademed Amazon

Amazona diadema (Spix) 1824, new
status (*Amazona autumnalis diadema*,
Forshaw 1973, etc.)

DESCRIPTION: Length 36 cm.; green;
under parts lighter green; forehead and
lores scarlet red; upper part of head to
nape and sides of neck green, each
feather edged in lilac blue; cheek and
ear region emerald green; wing feathers
green, red on the outer secondaries
forming a speculum; tail feathers
green; outer tail feathers red on the
outer vanes; iris orangish brown;
orbital ring white; cere pink; bill
yellowish, upper and lower mandibles
at times blackish brown on tomial
edges; toes grayish.

Youngsters: Head coloration less
intense; iris brown.

RANGE: Northwestern part of the
Brazilian state of Amazonas.

REMARKS: The author felt obliged to
treat the Diademed Amazon, which has
until now been classified as a
subspecies of the Red-lored Amazon
(*Amazona autumnalis*), as a separate
species. To be sure, this species
exhibits a very close kinship with
Amazona autumnalis salvini, but the
geographic separation of the ranges of
diadema and *salvini*, along with the
absence of an intermediate subspecies,
substantiates their independence.
Moreover, it must also be considered
that the subspecies of *Amazona
autumnalis* are all purely lowland birds;
therefore, an easterly expansion of their
ranges in Venezuela, Colombia, and
Ecuador is impossible because of the
geographic situation. The Cordillera de
Merida in Venezuela as well as the
Andes in Colombia and Ecuador form a
natural barrier.

The calls of the Diademed Amazon
have a different intonation. It is
known, of course, that within a species
the calls are affected by imprinted

differences; in a given area, flocks of related amazon parrots often develop characteristic call vocabularies—dialects, if you will. Nevertheless, the difference between the Diademed Amazon and the subspecies of the Red-lored Amazon is much greater.

WAY OF LIFE: The Diademed Amazon lives in a region which even today must be considered one of the least explored parts of the earth. While it is true that collectors and hunters penetrate the "green hell" again and again, their observations of the native animal and plant kingdoms extend as far as the banks of the navigable rivers.

The range of the Diademed Amazon lies between the Rio Negro and the Rio Solimoes in the northwestern part of the Brazilian state of Amazonas. Observations of this amazon-parrot species are not available for understandable reasons (impenetrable rain forest). The author has stayed in the tropical rain forest on several occasions and found that it is virtually hopeless to try to make extended observations of the animals. Sometimes one has the good fortune to discover an occupied nest cavity, so that one has the opportunity to observe the birds at the nest several times a day. Otherwise, one only sees the amazon parrots for brief moments, namely, as they fly away from the observer and immediately disappear among the treetops.

CARE AND BREEDING: The Diademed Amazon is very rarely kept in captivity. As a result of its isolated range in the Amazonian rain forest and, of course, the Brazilian ban on the exportation of animals, only single specimens of this amazon-parrot species occur in very few bird shipments from Peru and Ecuador.

Profile of a captive Red-lored Amazon, *Amazona autumnalis autumnalis*. Unlike *A. a. autumnalis*, the Diademed Amazon, *A. diadema*, is rarely kept by fanciers today.

Red-lored Amazon, *Amazona autumnalis.*

Indians, who take the amazon parrots from their nests and then rear them, often trade the hand-raised animals for life's necessities, so it is likely that the birds reach Peru and Ecuador by a tortuous route. They are bought by traders or their middlemen and are sent to Europe or North America.

Early in 1980, the author was able to purchase a Diademed Amazon accustomed to a cage from a private individual. Since no appropriate mate could be obtained, the Diademed Amazon was placed in an indoor flight with a Lilac-crowned Amazon (*Amazona finschi finschi*). On the basis

Top: A Red-lored Amazon stretching its neck to attain a better view. *Bottom:* Hand-taming is easily accomplished if begun at an early age. Red-lored Amazon, *Amazona autumnalis autumnalis.*

The floor was gnawed through the same day. After a new floor was put in, the 5-cm.-thick roof was attacked; in a very short time, she gnawed a hole approximately 13 cm. in diameter. After the completion of the new hole, the nest box was entered only through this opening.

The mate, the Lilac-crowned Amazon, showed no interest at all in the nest box. After the nest box was hung up, several matings were still observed but, unfortunately, egg laying did not take place. By the middle of June the "love life" had died down. In the meantime a fancier who owned a male Diademed Amazon was located, so the female Diademed Amazon now has a mate of her species. That the Diademed Amazon just mentioned was the loudest of all amazon parrots the author has owned should not be kept hidden. In the twilight hours particularly, the bird screeched at an unbearably high pitch.

of the shape of the head and bill, it was thought to be a female Diademed Amazon; the Lilac-crowned Amazon was a guaranteed male. The birds got along well from the start. Small fights, which never degenerated into viciousness, added spice to the lives of the two parrots. The Eclectus Parrots (*Eclectus roratus pectoralis*) housed in a nearby flight on the left were respected by the Diademed Amazon; in contrast, the young amazon parrots and Grey Parrots in the adjacent aviary on the right were attacked at once by the Diademed Amazon as soon as they came near the separating bars. Each attack by the amazon parrot was accompanied with a great outcry; also, the tail feathers were spread and the pupils were extremely contracted. Before and after such attacks, the Diademed Amazon made a very loud breathing sound. In May, after the two amazon parrots were together for a few weeks, the first mating attempts were observed. A tree trunk, about 70 cm. high, 50 cm. in diameter, and with an entrance hole of about 11 cm., was hung in the flight and was immediately accepted by the Diademed Amazon.

Red-lored Amazon looking bright and attentive.

Top: Bodin's Amazon, *Amazona festiva bodini,* a geographic race of the Festive Amazon, is found only rarely in the care of fanciers. *Bottom:* A wing-clipped Festive Amazon, *A. f. festiva.* Note that both the tail and wing feathers have been clipped.

Festive Amazon
Amazona festiva (Linnaeus) 1758 — 2 subspecies

1. *Amazona festiva festiva* (Linnaeus)

DESCRIPTION: Length approximately 35 cm.; green; nape feathers with dark edging; frontal band and lores dark red; forward part of cheek region turquoise blue; region behind eye and chin light blue; cheeks yellow green; lower back and rump red; carpal edge greenish yellow; primaries dark blue; secondaries green, blue on the inner vanes; primary coverts and alula blue;

underside of wing green; thigh yellow green; tail feathers green with yellowish green edging; outermost tail feathers blue on the outer vane; iris orange red; orbital ring gray; bill grayish black; feet gray.

Youngsters: Only a small amount of blue in the eye region and on the chin; lower back and rump green interspersed with a few red feathers; iris brown.

RANGE: Eastern Ecuador, northeastern Peru, and a large part of the Brazilian state of Amazonas.

2. *Amazona festiva bodini* (Finsch) — Bodin's Amazon

DESCRIPTION: Like the nominate subspecies, but more olive green; feathers on head, nape, and neck have dark edging; lores blackish, forehead red up to crown, changing into reddish lilac; forward cheek region turquoise blue; rear cheek region to ear coverts greenish blue; carpal edge yellow; primaries and secondaries green; outer primaries greenish black toward tips; primary coverts and alula green.

Youngsters: Blue and green areas on the head area restricted and less intensely colored; lower back and rump green interspersed with a few red feathers; iris brown.

RANGE: Northwestern Guyana and

impenetrable rain forests that grow in the tropical-zone lowlands. The vast rain forests and the extensive swampy areas scarcely permit careful observations in the wild. It is suspected that the Festive Amazon is the most numerous species of its genus along the upper Amazon River. The parrots dwell primarily in the high tree tops. In the late afternoon hours the small

Festive Amazon, *Amazona festiva festiva*. Besides eastern Ecuador and northeastern Peru, the range of this parrot includes a large portion of the Brazilian state of Amazonas.

the Venezuelan states of southern Amacuro and Bolívar.

REMARKS: Dr. O. Finsch named this amazon after Dr. Karl August Heinrich Bodinus (1814–1884). Dr. Bodinus was a renowned restorator as well as the director of the Berlin Zoological Gardens: *Chrysotis bodini finsch*, 1873.

WAY OF LIFE: The Festive Amazon lives along the Amazon River in the

flocks gather in their resting and roosting trees, and so may form relatively large assemblages.

The second subspecies, Bodin's Amazon, appears to be much rarer. The environment inhabited by them is in form and vegetation identical to that of the Festive Amazon. Along the Orinoco River in Bolivar, Venezuela, Bodin's Amazon can be found only

Distribution of the two *Amazona festiva* subspecies: (1) *A. f. festiva*; (2) *A. f. bodini*.

locally (Phelps and Phelps 1958). In northwestern Guyana, the birds have not been sighted for many years. It appears that in this region they occur only as wanderers for a short period.

The author was told by Hayden (1978) that near Kamarang, Guyana, near the Venezuelan border, two tame Bodin's, kept by an Indian tribe, could be seen. The two birds were about five months old. Since Hayden visited the Indians in August, it must be assumed that the amazon parrots had hatched in February or March.

CARE AND BREEDING: In the zoo in Port of Spain, Trinidad, the author was able to see a Bodin's Amazon (1979). The parrot was very tame, immediately came to the bars, and held out its head to be stroked. During the stroking it emitted a melodious humming sound.

Both Festive and Bodin's amazons are very rarely available in Germany. The author was able to see two handsome, extremely confiding Festive Amazons in the exquisite aviary of a North German fancier (1976). The two parrots were somewhat shy at first but soon became accustomed to their new surroundings, and took treats from the hand in no time at all. One of the amazons proved to be a talented talker and learned a repertoire of at least twenty words.

No reports of breeding exist, except for a hybrid breeding between a male Yellow-billed Amazon (*Amazona collaria*) and a female Bodin's Amazon.

Red-tailed Amazon
Amazona brasiliensis (Linnaeus)
1758

DESCRIPTION: Length approximately 37 cm.; green; forehead and lores orange red; occiput to nape changing from blue into green; turquoise beneath the lores as well as on the forward cheek region; ear region and chin steel blue; primaries and secondaries green, becoming blue toward tips; outer primaries blackish brown on the outer vanes; primary and secondary coverts green; greater under wing coverts yellow toward the tips; underside of wing yellow green; underside of the primaries and secondaries grayish green; carpal edge shows some red; upper tail coverts green, edged with yellow; tail feathers green, yellow green on the tips; outermost tail feathers red in the central part of the inner vane, the others red on the inner and outer vanes; central tail feathers lacking red; iris brown orange; orbital white; bill light horn color; feet gray brown.

Female: Like the male, but less extensive red on the forehead; cheeks and chin more bluish green; less extensive red on the carpal edge.

Youngsters: Like the adults, but duller head coloration; iris brown.

RANGE: Southeastern Brazil from southeastern São Paulo to Rio Grande do Sol.

REMARKS: It is very difficult to give a systematic place in the genus to the Red-tailed Amazon. A kinship with *Amazona rhodocorytha* can be recognized; however, intermediate forms between them are unknown. (See also *Amazona rhodocorytha* and *Amazona dufresniana*.)

WAY OF LIFE: The habitat favored by the Red-tailed Amazon is the formerly large *Araucaria* forests in the mountains near the coast in southeastern Brazil. Its range is

Tropical rain forest in the uplands of Guyana at an elevation of 500 meters above sea level.

virtually identical to those of the extremely rare Red-spectacled Amazon (*Amazona pretrei pretrei*) and the Vinaceous Amazon (*Amazona vinacea*). Outside the breeding season, all three of these threatened species often fly about together in small groups in search of food.

The accelerated clearing of forests in recent years threatens the survival of this magnificent amazon parrot. In the 1950s they were still found relatively frequently, but by 1969 Prof. Dr. Sick of the University of Rio de Janeiro declared the Red-tailed Amazon to be an endangered species.

At the beginning of 1964, Prof. Rossi della Riva saw three pairs of these amazons flying at a high altitude. The site of the observation was an isolated marshy area with sparse vegetation; only low undergrowth interspersed with small trees extended up the surrounding hills. The professor was able to observe the manner in which the Red-tailed Amazons flew into the

Distribution of *Amazona brasiliensis.*

nearby forests to feed. During the flight, but also while foraging in the forest, the birds were very loud. The parrots' nest sites, which were found after a thorough search, were located in the tops of dead palms in the open palm forest. One chick was found in one of the two nests discovered; three eggs lay in the other. The temperature in the amazon parrots' habitat ranges between 18 and 36°C, with an annual rainfall of up to 2000 mm.

Prof. Rossi della Riva's observations indicate that the courtship period and the search for a nest site begins in November, as with other parrots that live at the same latitude. The nestling period of the young thus ends in mid-to-late March. The search for food during the breeding season takes place in the vicinity of the nest tree. After the young are fledged, the birds wander locally, and in so doing can go as far as extreme southeastern Paraguay and Misiones in Argentina. In the *Araucaria* forests of southeastern Brazil, Red-tailed Amazons form small bands with the Red-spectacled Amazon (*Amazona pretrei pretrei*) and the Vinaceous Amazon (*Amazona vinacea*) to search for food.

CARE AND BREEDING: As early as 1828, a Red-tailed Amazon is said to have been kept in the collection of the Austrian emperor at Schönbrunn. In the following years, the birds were imported sporadically; in 1912 some reached the Berlin Zoo. Today, very few Red-tailed Amazons are in the possession of fanciers. It can be assumed with a great degree of certainty that there are no living specimens of this very attractively colored amazon parrot in central Europe.

Prof. Dr. Rossi della Riva succeeded in breeding this rare amazon parrot species in captivity in 1969, 1970, 1974, and 1975. Of course, the climatic conditions in Brazil contributed to this success.

The Red-tailed Amazon is listed in Appendix I of the Washington Convention.

Red-browed Amazon

Amazona rhodocorytha (Salvadori) 1890, new status (*Amazona dufresniana rhodocorytha*, Forshaw 1983, etc.)

DESCRIPTION: Length approximately 34 cm.; green, under parts lighter green; forehead, lores, and frontal band orange red, extending to occiput; yellow orange below the eye and forward cheek region, becoming green blue toward nape and chin; carpal edge yellow green; primaries dark blue; secondaries green, the outer three secondaries red toward base; tail feathers green, the outer tail feathers yellow green toward tip with orange red spot on the vane; iris orange red; orbital ring blue gray; upper mandible reddish, gray toward tip; lower mandible horn gray; toes grayish.

Youngsters: Orange-yellow feathers on the forehead, interspersed with green; iris brown.

RANGE: Eastern Brazil from Alagoas southward to Rio de Janeiro.

REMARKS: The Red-browed Amazon was classified as a subspecies of the Blue-cheeked Amazon until now. The

The Red-browed Amazon, *Amazona rhodocorytha*, was considered a subspecies of the Blue-cheeked Amazon, *A. dufresniana*, until further considerations of its range and plumage markings persuaded scientists to group it as an individual species.

Distribution of the Red-browed Amazon, *Amazona rhodocorytha*.

range of *A. rhodocorytha* as well as its plumage markings clearly argue against the previous treatment. Much more likely is a close kinship with the Red-tailed Amazon (*Amazona brasiliensis*); intermediate forms between the two species are lacking however, or such forms are still unknown. (See also *Amazona dufresniana* and *Amazona brasiliensis*).

WAY OF LIFE: The Red-browed Amazon is a very seriously threatened species in its range: the central Brazilian montane forests near the coast. The forests, which were still extensive at the turn of the century, were soon destroyed, ploughed up for immense coffee and cocoa plantations.

The coastal rain forests fell victim to dense human settlement. The constant felling of trees, as well as the great expansion of land used for raising cattle and farming, appreciably reduced the range of the Red-browed Amazon. Already in 1969, Prof. Dr. Sick listed this amazon parrot as an extremely endangered species, noting that in the Brazilian state of Rio de Janeiro, the southernmost part of its range, it had already been extirpated.

Although the Red-browed Amazon occurs in the vicinity of densely populated regions, there are virtually no observations in the wild from the last two decades. Just as little is known of its breeding behavior. No doubt this is additional proof of its continually decreasing population. Before 1950, Red-browed Amazons could still be observed in large flocks. In the period from June to September, in particular, the parrots were conspicuous in the coastal regions with mangroves. After this time, the birds withdrew in small parties into the mountainous backcountry.

No data exist concerning the breeding season of the Red-browed Amazon, but it can be assumed that it begins at the end of November or the beginning of December, and that it lasts until the young are fledged in March or April.

CARE AND BREEDING: The Red-browed Amazon was already very rare in zoos and in the aviaries of parrot fanciers even before it was listed in Appendix I of the Washington Convention (CITES). In the past, no doubt, the Red-browed Amazon was not identified correctly; it was simply called a "Red-fronted Amazon," like so many other species of its genus: *A. finschi, A. viridigenalis, A. autumnalis,* etc.

Years ago, the Walsrode bird park exhibited five of these very impressively colored amazon parrots to astonished visitors.

Single Red-browed Amazons have come into the hands of parrot fanciers in recent years. The majority of these birds had been kept in Brazil as cage birds and were then exported from the country with the permission of the Brazilian government. It is amazing how many rare animal species are kept by Brazilian natives. Amazon parrots, because of their talking ability, are in very high favor. To be sure, the methods of feeding and accommodation practiced are often very unsatisfactory.

The Red-browed Amazon is by nature a quiet, wary parrot, and accordingly an ideal cage and aviary bird. Unfortunately, because of the considerable threat to this amazon parrot in its environment, in the near future it will soon have completely disappeared from bird parks and breeders' aviaries. The author is prepared at any time to act as an intermediary in order to guarantee that the remaining singly kept birds can be brought together. Then at least there would be a slight chance of a brood or two in captivity, to promote the survival of this amazon parrot, which is listed in Appendix I of the Washington Convention (CITES).

Blue-cheeked Amazon
Amazona dufresniana (Shaw) 1812

DESCRIPTION: Length approximately 35 cm.; green; breast and belly lighter green; neck and back feathers have dark edging; frontal band and lores orange yellow; feathers on the forehead yellow, edged in green; cheeks and ear region violet blue to nape; carpal edge yellow green; primaries dark blue; secondaries green, the four outermost feathers yellow orange at the base, forming a speculum; underside of wing light green; tail feathers green, light green toward tip, the outer tail feathers yellow orange on the inner vanes to base; iris orange red; orbital ring gray; upper mandible reddish; lower mandible dark gray, horn colored toward tip; feet gray.

Youngsters: Orange-yellow feathers on the forehead interspersed with green; iris brown.

RANGE: Northernmost Pará in northeastern Brazil, French Guiana, Surinam, Guyana, and extreme eastern Venezuela.

REMARKS: The Blue-cheeked, or Dufresne's, Amazon was named after the French naval officer Nicolas Thomas Marion du Fresne (1729–?),

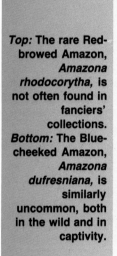

Top: **The rare Red-browed Amazon,** *Amazona rhodocorytha,* **is not often found in fanciers' collections.** *Bottom:* **The Blue-cheeked Amazon,** *Amazona dufresniana,* **is similarly uncommon, both in the wild and in captivity.**

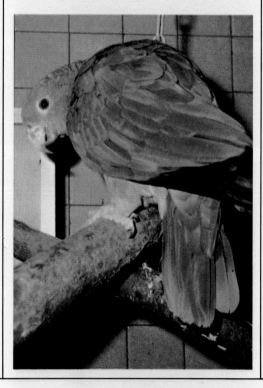

who in 1771 was ordered by the Marquis de Castries to search for new land in the South Seas: *Psittacus dufresnianus* 1812.

The Blue-cheeked Amazon, whose range primarily covers the Guyana states, has until now been treated as the nominate form of a species that included the subspecies *Amazona dufresniana rhodocorytha* (Red-browed Amazon). The author, on the basis of the differences in plumage coloration between the species, as well as the extreme geographic discontinuity of the ranges, adopts the view that both species have evolved in isolation over the course of millennia. Undoubtedly, the ranges of both species were more extensive in earlier times, but it can nevertheless be assumed that the two species never had direct contact with each other. (See also *Amazona rhodocorytha.*)

WAY OF LIFE: The Blue-cheeked Amazon is found in the tropical rain forests of the Guyana countries. Its environment stretches from the coastal zones consisting of mangrove swamps into the mountain ridges covered with impenetrable rain forests in the backcountry. The wet tropical climate with its minimal temperature fluctuations causes all "scientific curiosity" to falter, so that reports about the life in the wild of this amazon-parrot species are very few. Blue-cheeked Amazons are far rarer than, for example, the Orange-winged, Yellow-crowned, or Mealy amazons (*Amazona amazonica amazonica, A. ochrocephala ochrocephala, A. farinosa farinosa*) that occur in the same region. Hayden notified the author in 1978 that he was able to observe five Blue-cheeked Amazons foraging for food on the northern slope of Julianatops in the Wilhelmina mountains. Hayden was able to approach to within about 30 m., after which the birds flew silently away.

According to Hayden, the breeding season, as reported to him by natives, begins in February or March and ends after the nestling period of the young shortly before the start of the rainy season in May or June.

CARE AND BREEDING: Blue-cheeked Amazons are seldom in the animal trade. In 1980, the author discovered one Blue-cheeked Amazon among approximately 200 Orange-winged Amazons (*Amazona amazonica*) at an animal dealer's. The bird was quite tame and immediately came to the bars to have its head stroked.

In 1830, a Blue-cheeked Amazon was in the collection of the emperor of Austria.

The Red-browed Amazon inhabits montane forests near the coast of Brazil.

Distribution of *Amazona dufresniana.*

Vinaceous Amazon
Amazona vinacea (Kuhl) 1820

DESCRIPTION: Length approximately 32 cm.; green; occiput and back feathers with dark edging; lores and narrow frontal band dark red; nape and chin turquoise green; throat and breast wine-red lilac; belly feathers green, toward the base wine-red lilac; carpal edge orange; primaries green, toward tip blue on the outer vane; red speculum on the three outer secondaries; tail feathers green with yellow-green tips; outer tail feathers red at the base; iris reddish brown; orbital ring gray; bill reddish; upper mandible horn colored on ridge and tip; feet gray.

Female: Breast and belly plumage duller.

Youngsters: Few red feathers on frontal band and lores; wine-red lilac only on upper part of breast; bill horn colored, red at the base.

RANGE: Southeastern Brazil from southern Bahía southward to Rio Grande do Sul; northeastern Argentina in Misiones; southeastern Paraguay.

WAY OF LIFE: Vinaceous Amazons form small flocks with others of their own species outside of the breeding season. They readily flock together with related species, such as the Red-spectacled Amazon (*Amazona pretrei pretrei*) and the Red-tailed Amazon (*Amazona brasiliensis*). Wild Vinaceous Amazons have also been seen with Scaly-headed Parrots (*Pionus maximiliani maximiliani* and *P. m. siy*). The amazon parrots are native to the *Araucaria* forests (subtropical climatic zone), where they feed on the seeds when they ripen. Only a few years ago the birds were still relatively common in their range, but the heavy logging as well as the spread of agriculture led to an abrupt decline of the species. A Brazilian from Porto Alegre informed the author that he still regularly found Vinaceous Amazons a few years ago on his extended hiking trips in the coastal mountains. The Brazilian further reported that since 1977 he had not

Vinaceous Amazon, *Amazona vinacea*, found in southeastern Brazil, northeastern Argentina and southeastern Paraguay. The name Vinaceous refers to the wine-colored chest and throat coloration.

Despite an attractive coloration and hearty temperament, the Vinaceous Amazon is rarely seen in the hobby, due to its limited numbers and the restrictions on its exportation.

caught a glimpse of Vinaceous Amazons in this region. In the meantime, these amazon parrots were listed in Appendix I of the Washington Convention (CITES).

CARE AND BREEDING: As mentioned above, Vinaceous Amazons may no longer be traded and therefore are only very rarely offered by private fanciers.

Several years ago, the author was able to care for a Vinaceous Amazon for an extended period of time. Within a few days, although it was already at least five years old (recognizable by the somewhat scaly toes), the amazon parrot became hand-tame and immediately took treats offered by hand. When it felt threatened by other amazons kept in the same flight, it ruffled its nape feathers and produced growling noises. Otherwise it was quiet and reserved. Other Vinaceous Amazons proved to be very lively. A Vinaceous Amazon kept by an Austrian fancier, which was housed with other amazon parrots in an outdoor flight about 30 square meters, turned out to be the true master of the territory. Even Yellow-headed Amazons and Mealy Amazons (*A. ochrocephala oratrix* and *A. farinosa*), which, after all, are markedly larger, relinquished their

Vinaceous Amazons have proven capable breeders in captivity. Due to their limited numbers today, it is hoped that keepers of these parrots will make every effort possible to propagate the species.

places when the Vinaceous Amazon claimed them for itself.

Broods have been reared repeatedly. In 1971, two young are said to have been reared in England (Low 1973). A Swiss fancier (Poschung 1978) managed a successful breeding in 1978. In 1977, a mate was provided for a Vinaceous Amazon which had been obtained in 1975. After the two birds got on well from the first, and as they exhibited certain differences in coloration, it was assumed that they were a pair. In the spring of 1978, the birds were observed feeding each other. On the 20th of May a nest-box inspection led to a joyous surprise, for three eggs (measurements approximately 38.1 × 28.7 mm.) were discovered. After the female began incubating, nest-box inspections were conducted only weekly. On the 21st of June, a chick approximately 6 cm. long lay in the nest. The second youngster hatched three days later. Unfortunately, the bird that hatched first died on the 21st of July. Worst of all, on the 27th of July the female perished as well, and all hopes of successfully rearing the remaining youngster shrank to zero. After the male continued to feed the little parrot, a glimmer of hope stirred that the youngster could nevertheless still be reared. In addition, the bird was fed a pap. From this time on the youngster developed splendidly. It showed itself, being about 21 cm. long, at the entrance hole on the 15th of August, and on the 25th of August outside the nest box. Thus despite the greatest difficulties during the nestling period, success could still be achieved. In order to ensure the future survival of the beautiful Vinaceous Amazon among fanciers, it would be very welcome if the owners of these birds would join into breeders' associations. Only in this way will it be possible to prevent this amazon parrot from completely disappearing from European aviaries.

Distribution of *Amazona vinacea*. Note that the distribution does not extend beyond the south or southwestern Brazilian border.

Red-spectacled Amazon
Amazona pretrei (Temminck)
1830 — 2 subspecies

1. *Amazona pretrei pretrei*
(Temminck) 1830

DESCRIPTION: Length 32 cm.; green; nape, back, breast, and belly feathers have dark edging; forehead, lores, eye region red; isolated red feathers on the cheek; bend of wing, wing coverts, and carpal edge red; primaries and secondaries green, blue toward tip; tail feathers green, yellow green toward the tips, the three outer tail feathers have a red spot at the base on the inner vane; thigh red; iris orange; orbital ring white; bill yellowish; feet yellowish brown.

Youngsters: Only a few red feathers on the forehead, lores, and eye region; bend of wing and carpal edge green.

RANGE: Southeastern Brazil from southern São Paulo to Rio Grande do Sul, Misiones in northeastern Argentina, extreme southeastern Paraguay, and possibly northern Uruguay.

REMARKS: C. J. Temminck showed his regard for the great diligence and skill of the wildlife artist Jean Gabriel Pretre (1800–1840), who was employed at the Museum d'Histoire Naturelle, Paris, by naming the Red-spectacled Amazon after him: *Psittacus pretrei*.

2. *Amazona pretrei tucumana*
(Cabanis) 1885 — Tucuman Amazon

DESCRIPTION: Length approximately 31 cm.; darker green; feathers have more pronounced edging; red only on forehead and in speculum; red absent from tail feathers; thigh yellow.

Youngsters: Thigh green.

RANGE: Southeastern Bolivia and Chuquisaca; northwestern and northeastern Argentina: from Jujuy, Salta, and Tucuman to Chaco and Misiones.

REMARKS: Based on the latest findings and studies—definitive results do not yet exist—one may conclude that the subspecies *Amazona pretrei tucumana* should be considered a separate species: *Amazona tucumana*. In some of the foreign-language literature the subspecies is already treated as a separate species.

WAY OF LIFE: Both subspecies of *Amazona pretrei* are birds that principally live in subtropical and temperate climates. The Red-spectacled Amazon is indigenous to the large *Araucaria* forests (*Araucaria excelsa*); the Tucuman Amazon inhabits

Rich, dense Brazilian flora in bloom.

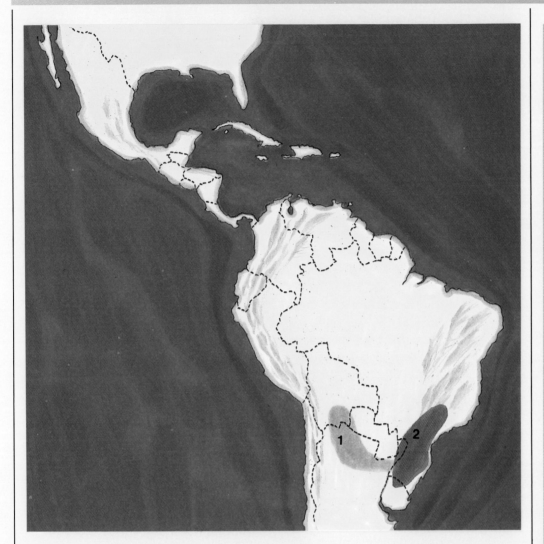

Distribution of the two *Amazona pretrei* subspecies: (1) *A. p. tucumana*; (2) *A. p. pretrei*.

alder forests (*Alnus jorullensis*). The extensive clearing of the evergreen forests in recent decades have markedly reduced the habitat of the amazon parrots; as a result *Amazona pretrei pretrei* had to be listed in Appendix I of the Washington Convention (CITES).

J. M. Forshaw reports that in 1971 he was able to observe Red-spectacled Amazons in the vicinity of Vacaria, Rio Grande do Sul, Brazil. The region was made up of rolling, open grassland, which was divided by valleys almost completely covered with dense *Araucaria* forest, which is where the birds lived. He saw thousands of parrots, which gathered in the groups of trees surrounding a marsh before

they flew to roost in a nearby site in the forest. The number of birds present was estimated at between 10,000 and 30,000. A farmer, on whose land a congregation site of the parrots was located, stated that some parrots lived there the year round, but that the vast majority came in April to feed on the ripe *Araucaria* seeds, and would depart in July.

J. M. Forshaw reports further that from late afternoon until long after sundown, small flocks again and again flew over the open grassland to the assembly site, and sometimes stopped in the forested valleys. From a hill one could observe very well the gathering place as well as the parrots flying by.

The difference between adults and juveniles could be seen clearly. It appeared that many of the flocks were family groups. In the trees, the parrots were very active, and it was difficult to approach them. Often thousands of parrots took wing and circled over the treetops, during which they made an indescribable racket. Forshaw describes the event as an extraordinarily impressive spectacle. After the onset of darkness, the amazon parrots flew to the roosting trees. The powerful, energetic flight, which is characterized by shallow, rapid wing beats as well as by erratic turns and somersaults, is a very interesting sight.

Tucuman Amazons live mainly on the eastern slopes of the Andes to an elevation of 2000 m. The parrots occur in the northeastern Argentine provinces of Chaco and Misiones only outside the breeding season. Both subspecies seem to lead a very nomadic life. This behavior can be linked to the climatic conditions that obtain in the parrots' range. There are the four seasons, with a spring, summer, fall, and winter that resemble central Europe with respect to climate and vegetation. The breeding season of the amazon parrots begins in the spring, the months of October and November, and lasts into the months of January and February, at the conclusion of the nestling period. After the young become self-sufficient, the amazons wander through the quite sparsely settled landscape, following the ripening stands of seeds, particularly aspens and *Araucarias*, and also other stands of fruit.

Reports concerning the breeding habits are very meager. In 1943, it is reported that at Padilla, Chuquisaca, Bolivia, a captured bird (female Tucuman Amazon) was incubating four eggs, approximately 34.5 × 26.7 mm.

If future logging in the range of the Red-spectacled and Tucuman amazons extends over a large area, one must face the possibility that in a few years the endangered birds will completely lose their habitat, which has been intact for centuries.

CARE AND BREEDING: The Red-spectacled Amazon, with its brilliant red wing covert feathers, is an extremely rare bird among bird fanciers. It can be assumed that neither in Europe nor in North America are these birds to be found in captivity. In *Die Gefiederte Welt* 18:29 (1899), it is mentioned that Fräulein Hagenbeck showed a bird of this species at the Ornis Exhibition in Berlin.

The zoo in Porto Alegro, Brazil, had a pair of these rare birds. After the local government of Rio Grande do Sul informed the zoo personnel of the endangered status of this species in the wild, special efforts on the part of the zoo administration were undertaken in order to obtain young from this amazon-parrot pair. Whether this resulted in a successful breeding, however, is not known to the author.

The subspecies *A. p. tucumana* is also a bird rarely kept in captivity. However, beginning in 1979, small shipments of this subspecies arrived in Germany time and again, and a majority of the birds imported were purchased by experienced parrot breeders. Importers informed the author that the Tucuman Amazon was very susceptible to illness during the acclimation period. The cause of the illness of the birds, as is true with the majority of other imported parrots, should certainly be sought in the poor feeding methods overseas. Often the animals sit at the exporter's for weeks or even months at a time, during which they are fed extremely one-sidedly, usually with corn alone. Understandably, the body loses substance during this period. The subsequent quarantine period with the legally mandated feeding practices

further weakens the amazons; that high mortality rates in the birds often results is unavoidable with this diet and is most regrettable.

Well-acclimated Tucuman Amazons are agreeable charges, and soon lose their shyness if treated in a suitable manner. Without hesitation one can permit them, provided that they have not been accustomed to too warm a temperature, to spend the entire day in the flight outdoors on warmer winter days.

T. Silva of the United States and Jacobsen of Denmark informed the author that successful breeding of the Tucuman Amazon took place in the United States in 1981. Further details, however, were not provided.

Aerial view of the meeting of the Rio Negro and the Amazon River in South America.

White-fronted Amazon
Amazona albifrons (Sparrman)
1788 —4 subspecies

1. *Amazona albifrons albifrons* (Sparrman)

DESCRIPTION: Length approximately 26 cm.; green; nape and back feathers with darker green edging; ventral feathers light green, light dark edging; narrow frontal band, lores, and eye region red; forehead white, sometimes light yellowish; crown bluish green changing to green on occiput; outer primaries at the tips of the outer vanes blackish blue, then blue, becoming green toward base; inner primaries as well as secondaries blue on the outer vanes; all primaries and secondaries brownish black on the inner vanes; primary coverts and alula red; underside of wing bluish green; tail feathers green, yellow green toward tip; outer tail feathers red at the base of the inner vanes; bill yellowish; iris orange; orbital ring light gray; toes yellowish brown-gray.

Female like male, but red facial area less extensive; primary coverts and alula green; blue on primaries and secondaries not as intense.

In juveniles, sex is immediately recognizable from the different wing coloration; the red of the facial mask stops above and below the eye; the cere and orbital ring are virtually white; iris dark brown.

RANGE: Mexico along the Pacific coast from Nayarit southward to southwestern Guatemala.

2. *Amazona albifrons saltuensis* (Nelson)

DESCRIPTION: Like the nominate subspecies, but blue green on the crown extending to nape.

RANGE: Mexico from southern Sinaloa and southwestern Durango along the Pacific coast to southern Sonora.

Pair of White-fronted Amazons, *Amazona albifrons albifrons*, in an outdoor aviary. These birds are inhabitants of dry scrub and deciduous forests and avoid the moist tropical lowlands and rain forests.

Male White-fronted Amazon, *Amazona albifrons albifrons*. The specific sex character, the red alula on the wing, can be seen clearly. The red eye mask is not as yet clearly demarcated from the other parts of the plumage.

The White-fronted Amazon is particularly populous on the steep Pacific coast of Mexico; its range extends from Nayarit southward to southwestern Guatemala.

3. *Amazona albifrons nana* (W. de W. Miller)

DESCRIPTION: Like the nominate subspecies, but breast and belly feathers have darker edging; ear region darker green; somewhat smaller.

RANGE: Mexico along the Gulf and Caribbean coasts from southeastern Veracruz through parts of the Yucatan peninsula southward to northwestern Costa Rica.

4. *Amazona albifrons xantholora* (G. R. Gray), new status (*Amazona xantholora*, Forshaw 1973) — Yellow-lored Amazon

DESCRIPTION: Like the nominate subspecies, but darker green and all feathers have dark edging; lores yellow gold; narrow frontal band yellow gold; ear patch blackish green; alula green.

The sex of juveniles is immediately recognizable by the different wing coloration; forehead and frontal band blue green; only isolated red feathers in the facial mask.

RANGE: Southeastern Mexico on the Yucatan peninsula in the states of southern Yucatan, Quintana Roo, and southeastern Campeche; the island of Cozumel; Belize; and the island of Roatán off Honduras.

REMARKS: The author regards the Yellow-lored Amazon as a subspecies of *Amazona albifrons*. Until now the Yellow-lored Amazon was treated as a separate species, *Amazona xantholora*, but its sex-specific characters, which are not as pronounced in any other amazon-parrot species, clearly support the classification of *xantholora* as a subspecies of *Amazona albifrons*. Outside the breeding season, the birds wander and then advance into the range of *Amazona albifrons nana*.

Examination of several museum specimens from El Salvador and Honduras revealed evident differences in wing coloration. The specimens from El Salvador exhibited coloration characteristic of *A. a. albifrons* (not like *A. a. nana*), having a bluish green underside of the wing. The specimens from Honduras (Rio Lindo, 500 m.), on the other hand, were green on the underside of the wing. The primaries

had only a slight amount of blue on the tips of the outer vanes; the rest of the outer vane was light green. The red feathers of the primary coverts were all green at the tip. Unfortunately, only a very limited number of skins from El Salvador and Honduras were at the author's disposal, and material from Nicaragua and Costa Rica was completely lacking, so that one could not obtain complete data. It is entirely conceivable that in the southern part of the range, beside *nana*, an additional subspecies, intermediate between *nana* and *xantholora*, occurs, or that *nana* is replaced by another subspecies in this region.

WAY OF LIFE: The subspecies *albifrons*, *saltuensis*, and *nana* are birds of the dry scrub and deciduous forests. The moist tropical lowlands and the rain forests are avoided by these subspecies or are visited only occasionally. In southern Sonora, they are seen in dry districts overgrown with cacti. The subspecies *xantholora* favors hot, wet regions to live in.

The White-fronted Amazon is always numerous on the steep Pacific coast in Mexico. The subspecies *nana*, which inhabits the eastern coast of Central America, appears not to be as abundant; at least it is not as easy to track down, since the birds are at times localized in the moderately high rain forests. The landscapes on the Yucatan peninsula in which White-fronted Amazons occur seem to be clearly different from those inhabited by the Yellow-lored Amazon. Klass, to be sure, reports that he sighted a large mixed flock of White-fronted and Yellow-lored Amazons in the town of Champoton in the province of Campeche in 1968. The author, however, questions this assertion, since it seems impossible to distinguish the two amazon-parrot subspecies at a distance. Paynter was able to discover

only Yellow-lored Amazons near Champoton. Russel (1964) indicates that this bird species occurs very rarely in Belize; instead, he observed that *xantholora* was more common in what was formerly British Honduras. The habitats favored by *nana* here too differ from those of *xantholora*.

Outside the breeding season the birds wander outside of their normal range and move into those of other subspecies. For the breeding season the animals then return to the breeding range. De Grahl considers the breeding range of *xantholora* to be limited to Quintana Roo (Mexico) and Belize. The breeding range of *nana* adjoins these regions. It is believed that the range of *nana* covers the western and northern portion of the Yucatan peninsula, while *xantholora* occurs in the southeastern portions of the peninsula. Paynter (1955), near the

Head study of a White-fronted Amazon, *Amazona albifrons.* The characteristic white forehead, which is the basis for the name, is clearly visible. On the other hand, because of the red eye ring it has also been called the Spectacled Amazon.

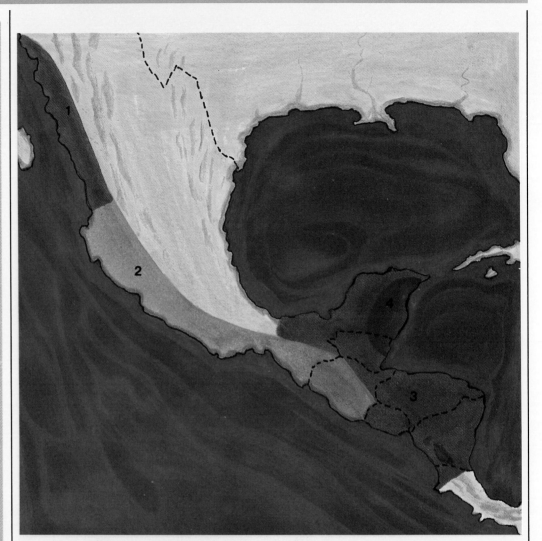

Distribution of the four *Amazona albifrons* subspecies: (1) *A. a. saltuensis*; (2) *A. a. albifrons*; (3) *A. a. nana*; (4) *A. a. xantholora*.

town of Champoton on the Gulf of Mexico, in the state of Campeche, was able to observe at least 1500 birds and to approach them very closely. He was never able to observe *xantholora* together with *nana*. The favored habitat of the amazon was mixed deciduous and pine forests. The same roosting trees were used by entire flocks for a fairly long period. At sunrise, small parties dispersed in different directions in search of food. At sunset, they returned to the habitual roosting trees. On the island of Cozumel, the birds appear as a result of daily trips from the mainland, which is about 15 km. away. Griscom (1926) observed that flocks of different sizes

flew from the mainland to the island every morning, dispersed on the island, and flew back to Quintana Roo in the evening. Nest trees could not be found on Cozumel. They do not seem to be as abundant in Belize. In 1947, a bird was captured on the island of Roatán, off Honduras. Here their occurrence is limited to the hilly pine forests.

The breeding season of the Yellow-lored Amazon falls in the dry months of March to June. In Belize, four nests were once located in Belize in the months of April and May.

The range of *A. a. albifrons* stretches southward to southern Guatemala and the border of Honduras and El

These two Yellow-lored Amazons, *Amazona albifrons xantholora* (formerly *A. xantholora*), are not yet fully colored. The bird perched on the left does not have the complete extension of the red area of plumage. The bird on the right is a male youngster in its first year and possesses the typical juvenile plumage and dark brown iris.

Salvador. El Salvador, Honduras, Nicaragua, and northwestern Costa Rica are supposedly inhabited by *nana*. The author's investigations (see REMARKS), suggest that it is entirely possible that *nana* is replaced by another subspecies in this region.

As a rule, the amazon parrots are found in lowlands, but also occur at elevations of up to 1800 m. The breeding season begins approximately in March in the southern parts of the range, and approximately in April or May in northwestern Mexico. The incubation period lasts 25–26 days, the nestling period about 7–8 weeks. The somewhat rounded eggs are approximately 30.3 × 22.7 mm. After the breeding and rearing season ends, the family groups assemble into small flocks. In the evening hours, the birds fly to the so-called roosting trees, which are also sought out by other flocks. Often over a thousand amazon parrots can be present at such meeting places; they can be detected from a considerable distance because of the great din. In the morning they again split up into small flocks in order to go in search of food. The four subspecies of the White-fronted Amazon feed primarily on palm fruits, berries, leaf and flower buds, figs, as well as cultivated fruits, corn, and grain. They can do considerable damage when they invade plantations. During feeding periods as well as the midday hours, the animals are extremely quiet; on the other hand, during flight their vocalizations, which have a harsh, metallic sound, are very loud.

CARE AND BREEDING: More often in recent years, the White-fronted subspecies *albifrons* and *saltuensis* have reached Germany and are for sale sporadically in the animal trade. Although they are very attractively colored, they are not so readily purchased by those buyers who wish to keep an amazon parrot that can learn to talk as a cage bird. The small size of this amazon parrot probably also is a factor here. Blue-fronted or Orange-winged amazons, which are certainly distinctly larger, and are in general also better known, are preferred. White-fronted Amazons obtained as youngsters are by nature just as amiable as their larger relatives. The mimicking talent is not as pronounced as in, for example, a Yellow-crowned Amazon. It should be noted, however, that there is very little information about their talking ability; received opinions should therefore not be generalized. Very young animals, which do not yet have the yellow forehead, can often be found on the market. For keeping singly and taming, these animals are always preferable to older members of the species. This is in general true of all amazon-parrot species.

In 1977, a German breeder effected what is apparently the first European breeding. The first breeding success of all is said to have occurred in Japan in 1922. In the United States a youngster was reared in 1948. Müller, the German breeder, housed a pair of White-fronted Amazons, among others, in a greenhouse under conditions of very high humidity. In March, a courtship period of about 14 days began. During this time the birds were especially noisy. The eggs were laid on the 27th and 29th of May. Nest-box inspection was virtually impossible because of the female's aggressiveness. On the 26th of June, a soft peeping could be heard coming from the nest box. The breeding pair were kept at bay and the nest box inspected. A well-fed youngster, a dead bird, and an infertile egg were discovered. In the youngster's fourth week of life it was discovered that the right foot was slightly crooked and the right wing was underdeveloped. In addition, the little parrot had very few down feathers. It was suspected that because of the one-sided feeding of the adults before breeding—during this time they consumed only seeds but no vegetables or fruit—the symptoms of deficiency were evident in the youngster. An injury, however, could also have occurred in the first days of life. After the fourth week, the female no longer spent the night in the nest box. It was therefore possible to administer a supplementary vitamin preparation to the youngster. On the 28th of August, the little amazon parrot left the nest box well feathered, and continued to be fed by the female. It was driven off by the male, and a few days later even chased and bitten. As a result, with injured wings and foot, the youngster had to be removed.

A further breeding success was achieved by a Swiss breeder named Böni in 1979. During the feeding carried out on the 24th of February, it was noticed that the female was breathing abnormally heavily. When the observer left the aviary, the breathing was again normal. When the aviary was entered again, the abnormal breathing process was repeated (moreover, this feigned difficulty in breathing was also observed with the German breeding pair; the author was also able to note the same with a Diademed Amazon). As a result, the nest box (30 × 30 × 50 cm., with entrance-hole diameter of 9 cm.) was examined immediately. To the greatest surprise, two eggs were observed. The eggs were 38 mm. long, had a diameter of 26 mm., weighed 10 g., and differed markedly from the size given by Schönwetter (1964).

On the 27th of February a third egg lay in the box. In the inspection carried out on the 3rd of March, it was seen that at least one egg was fertile. Consequently, the temperature in the aviary was raised to 18–20°C and the humidity to 80%. The first peeping was

detected on the 23rd of March. Since the female presumably started incubating after laying the third egg, an incubation period of approximately 26 days is indicated. The second youngster hatched two days later. The first feather sheaths broke through after 18–20 days. After 28 days, they

were already relatively well feathered, particularly on the wings. The first youngster left the nest on May 11, and the second followed on May 12. The nestling period thus lasted about 50 days.

The male, having cared for the young very well during the nestling period, also continued to provide food after they left the nest. The sex of the

Pair of White-fronted Amazons, *Amazona albifrons albifrons*. The bird on the left is a young female, and the bird on the right is a male. White-fronted Amazons have been bred successfully in captivity since 1977.

Amazona albifrons albifrons in an outdoor aviary at a bird park. Smaller than many other amazon parrots, the White-fronted Amazon has fared relatively well in captivity.

youngsters could be determined immediately; the male bird had red, the female green, primary coverts and alula. It should be noted that the breeding hen had only the innermost toe on her left foot and despite this handicap was fully capable of breeding.

The subspecies *xantholora* is very rare in captivity, and they are probably also mistaken for the nominate form in most cases. The zoological garden in Berlin was in possession of a Yellow-lored Amazon during the First World War. In 1977, three male and one female Yellow-lored Amazons reached a Swiss fancier (Meier 1980) from Germany. The Yellow-lored Amazons were housed with one male and three female White-fronted Amazons in a 3.0 × 2.3 m. flight. A constant temperature of 25°C and a humidity of 60–80% prevailed in the aviary. On June 20, 1980, it was noticed during the daily feeding that the female Yellow-lored Amazon had stayed in a nest. In an inspection carried out on August 4 at least three eggs were seen. The first two young hatched on August 15. On August 22, three large and one small chick as well as an additional egg were seen. High humidity prevailed in the nest box because the hen took part in the daily "rain bath" and returned to the nest box with wet plumage. On the 31st of August the three young that hatched first opened their eyes; the feather sheaths also gradually broke through. On September 11, after about the fourth week of life, one could already recognize from the primary coverts that there were three males and one female (the primary coverts are red in the cocks and green in the hens).

It is worth mentioning that, besides the breeding pair, there were also two Yellow-lored and four White-fronted amazons in the flight; no fighting that might have endangered the breeding developed. The author nevertheless holds the opinion that so-called community breeding always entails a definite risk. When one considers that a pair ready for breeding comes into breeding condition two to three weeks before the other pairs kept in the same flight, and then have already laid eggs in the nest box by the time the other pairs begin courtship, it may be assumed that the breeding effort of the first pair will be markedly disrupted. Under certain circumstances there may be fighting over the nest sites, in the course of which eggs already laid or even hatched youngsters may be harmed.

Cuban Amazon
Amazona leucocephala (Linnaeus)
1758 — 5 subspecies

1. *Amazona leucocephala leucocephala* (Linnaeus)

DESCRIPTION: Length approximately 32 cm.; green, dark edging; forehead and eye region white; chin, throat, and cheeks pinkish red; isolated pinkish red feathers spread over the breast; ear patch black; belly wine red, dark edging; primaries, secondaries, primary coverts, and alula blue; outer wing coverts blue on outer vane; underside of wing blue green; narrow red edging on the underside of the bend of the wing; tail feathers yellow green, outer tail feathers red on the base of the inner vane; iris reddish brown; orbital ring white; bill uniformly horn color; feet yellow brown.

Female: Like the male, but the narrow red edging on the underside of the bend of the wing absent or barely suggested.

Youngsters: Without or with only very little dark feather edging; belly without or with only very few wine-red feathers.

RANGE: Eastern and central Cuba.

2. *Amazona leucocephala palmarum* (Todd) — Isle of Pines Amazon

DESCRIPTION: Like the nominate subspecies, but darker green; throat darker pinkish red; belly darker wine red.

RANGE: Western portion of Cuba and the Isle of Pines.

3. *Amazona leucocephala caymanensis* (Cory) — Grand Cayman Amazon

DESCRIPTION: Like the nominate subspecies, but more yellow green; white on head less extensive; chin and throat more reddish; red on belly less extensive; somewhat larger.

RANGE: Grand Cayman Island.

4. *Amazona leucocephala hesterna* (Bangs) — Cayman Brac Amazon

DESCRIPTION: Like the nominate subspecies, but more yellow green; belly patch more extensive and intensely wine red; chin, throat, and cheeks richer pinkish red; somewhat smaller.

RANGE: The islands of Little Cayman and Cayman Brac.

5. *Amazona leucocephala bahamensis* (Bryant) — Bahaman Amazon

Headstudy of a fully colored Isle of Pines Amazon, *Amazona leucocephala palmarum*, whose range includes western Cuba and the Isle of Pines.

The Cuban Amazon, *Amazona leucocephala*, is fully protected on its native island of Cuba, the largest island of the Greater Antilles. Despite the large-scale agricultural development of Cuba's extensive lowlands, the Cuban Amazon still inhabits a relatively secure living space.

DESCRIPTION: Like the nominate subspecies, but the wine-red belly patch present only slightly or not at all; more extensive white on the forehead as well as around the eye region; somewhat larger.

RANGE: Once distributed over several islands of the Bahamas; today found only on Great Inagua and possibly Abaco.

WAY OF LIFE: The Cuban Amazon, with its five subspecies, has a very extended range. The nominate form as well as *palmarum* (which is also synonomized with the nominate form) occur on Cuba as well as the Isle of Pines, which is situated to the southwest. Cuba, with a width of 50–150 km. and a length of about 1200 km., is the largest island of the Greater Antilles. Extensive lowlands, which

make up about 75% of the land area, are the principal landforms. These lowlands, which were covered with moist forests in previous centuries, are today heavily used for agriculture and industry. Nevertheless, some parts of the environment are still relatively untouched and thus far have provided the Cuban Amazons, which are completely protected in Cuba, with a secure living space. The temperatures are constant and even at night do not fall below 20°C. The humidity is constantly high. Cuban Amazons inhabit all kinds of landforms. O. H. Garrido and A. Schwartz (1968) state that in the Guanahacabibes peninsula located in the western part of Cuba (a pure lowland region) the amazon parrots are quite numerous and are conspicuous because of their loud screeching. In previous years, the amazon parrots were hunted very intensively when they invaded orchards or other cultivated regions. Today, amazon parrots may not be shot or traded. Apparently the population on Cuba, because of the complete protection, has recovered to such an extent that it is no longer in any way threatened.

On the other hand, the survival of the remaining subspecies, which occur on the islands Grand Cayman, Little Cayman, Cayman Brac, Great Inagua, and possibly on Abaco, is very much in doubt. Unfortunately, there are still "sportsmen" who hunt these birds for amusement and in so doing will doubtless soon wipe out the small population remaining. In 1969, less than a thousand individuals of the subspecies *bahamensis* remained on Great Inagua (Fisher 1969). The Inagua Islands, which are located to the east of Cuba and have an area of 1446 sq. km., are very sparsely populated: about 1200 inhabitants (the Windsor Lake preserve holds the largest flamingo colony on earth). On the other islands of the Bahamas, this subspecies was sighted only once on Abaco. It must be noted here that approximately 700 islands of the most variable size belong to the Bahaman archipelago, only about 20 of which are inhabited. It is entirely possible that the Bahaman subspecies also occurs on other islands, but no data substantiate this. The subspecies *caymanensis* and *hesterna* live in the dry lowlands in the interior of the islands. A direct threat to their existence does not appear to exist, although the available habitat is only a few square kilometers in extent. Nevertheless, Noegel estimates that the population now consists of only 40–50 individuals.

The breeding season of the Cuban Amazon begins in March and lasts until the fledging of the young in August. The nest cavities, located at a height of about 6 m. above the ground and higher, are used repeatedly. As a rule, three to four eggs, 35 × 28 mm., are laid. The nestling period of the young lasts about 60–70 days. Once the young are reared, the family units again combine into flocks.

A yellow Cuban Amazon which was shot in Cuba in 1939 is found in the collection of the Cuban Academy of Science in the capital, Havana. All otherwise green-colored feathers are yellow in this specimen. The other

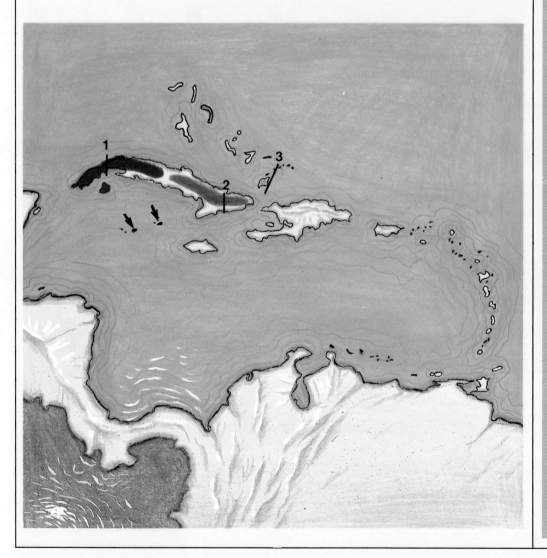

Distribution of the five *Amazona leucocephala* subspecies: (1) *A. l. palmarum*; (2) *A. l. leucocephala*; (3) *A. l. bahamensis*; (➤ east) *A. l. hasterna*; (➤ west) *A. l. caymanensis*.

colored areas exhibit no divergence.

CARE AND BREEDING: The nominate form of the Cuban Amazon was imported relatively frequently in the last century. Today it is encountered very seldom. Only a few fanciers and zoos possess these rare amazon parrots. Because of the political situation, Cuban Amazons are kept more often in the countries of Eastern Europe. For the most part, amazon parrots bred in the Havana zoo are sent to Eastern

apparently reared by her. The subspecies *bahamensis* is said to have been bred by an English breeder in 1909. From three eggs one youngster hatched, which unfortunately soon died.

In Japan, a successful breeding is said to have taken place in the breeding facility of Prince Taka-Tsukasa in 1922.

The Keston Farm in England was able to report the rearing of two youngsters in 1956. They were plucked

Group of Grand Cayman Amazons, *Amazona leucocephala caymanensis*, convening on a natural branch in their outdoor aviary.

European zoos. Eastern European visitors to Cuba occasionally have had the opportunity to take birds out of the country, and by this means were able to build up a small aviary stock. Dr. K. Russ reports that already in 1885 a hybrid between a Blue-fronted (*Amazona aestiva*) and a Cuban amazon was bred. In 1886 a youngster was again reared from the same pair. The egg was placed under a female Eclectus Parrot, and the youngster was

by the parents after they left the nest. Once separated from the parents, the feathers soon grew back.

In the Havana zoo, youngsters are regularly reared and then given to Eastern European zoos and fanciers or returned to the wild.

An additional breeding occurred in Czechoslovakia in 1975 (Bernasek 1976). Here, in May, always at intervals of two days, three eggs were laid, all of which were fertile (the shell of one egg was pushed in, and it had to be removed). On the 26th day of incubation, one egg had been pipped, and a youngster hatched from it on the 28th. The youngster was fed well by the parents until the third week of life, but subsequently had to placed under a pair of Cockatiels, which had a brood at the same time. The Cockatiels fed the amazon parrot until their own young were fledged. From the seventh to the tenth week, spoon feeding was undertaken by the keeper. After the tenth week of life, the little Cuban Amazon was virtually self-sufficient and was given supplementary feedings only occasionally. In the meantime, additional broods, with variable results, have been produced in other Eastern European countries.

In Germany, Cuban Amazons are quite scarce; many fanciers keep only single birds. It must therefore be expected that these attractively colored amazon parrots will soon have disappeared from aviaries if fanciers do not get together and undertake breeding attempts with Cuban Amazons, possibly in facilities operated by breeders' associations.

In Florida, Ramon Noegel has concerned himself with the keeping and breeding of amazon parrots for many years, concentrating on the Caribbean species and subspecies. All of the Cuban Amazons are housed separately by subspecies, to prevent interbreeding of the subspecies, that is, hybridization. There have already been successful breedings of the subspecies *leucocephala*, *palmarum*, and *caymanensis*. It is interesting that a female bred in captivity, which has been paired with an older cock, has already reared three young in her third year of life.

In an article in *Gef. Welt*, Vol. XVIII, No. 7 (1889) pp 69–71, 83, it is stated by P. Hieronymus that a pair of Eclectus Parrots (*Eclectus roratus*

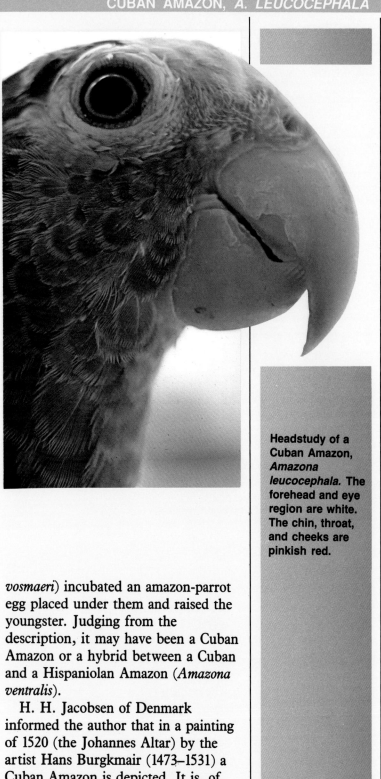

Headstudy of a Cuban Amazon, *Amazona leucocephala*. The forehead and eye region are white. The chin, throat, and cheeks are pinkish red.

vosmaeri) incubated an amazon-parrot egg placed under them and raised the youngster. Judging from the description, it may have been a Cuban Amazon or a hybrid between a Cuban and a Hispaniolan Amazon (*Amazona ventralis*).

H. H. Jacobsen of Denmark informed the author that in a painting of 1520 (the Johannes Altar) by the artist Hans Burgkmair (1473–1531) a Cuban Amazon is depicted. It is, of course, most remarkable that, a few years after the discovery of the West Indian islands and the American continents, a parrot indigenous to this region serves to illustrate a work of art created in central Europe.

Hispaniolan Amazon
Amazona ventralis (P. L. S. Müller) 1776

DESCRIPTION: Length approximately 28 cm.; green, with dark edging; forehead and lores white; crown and front of cheek region dark blue, black edging; ear patch black; isolated pinkish red feathers on the chin; belly dark wine red; primaries blue, black towards tip; secondaries blue, green on the outer vane; underside of wing blue green; tail feathers green, yellow green towards tip; outer tail feather red and yellow on the inner vane towards base, blue on the outer vane; orbital ring white; iris brown; bill light horn color; feet flesh color.

Youngsters: Duller plumage, only isolated wine-red feathers on the belly; iris dark brown.

RANGE: Dominican Republic, Haiti, and several of the small islands belonging to these countries, as well as Puerto Rico.

WAY OF LIFE: The Hispaniolan Amazon lives on the West Indian island of Hispaniola (with the countries of Haiti in the west and the Dominican Republic in the east) and several small neighboring Antillean islands. Hispaniola lies in the subtropics, where the average annual temperature is 26°C. Several mountain ranges running from the northwest to the southeast traverse the island, separated from one another by lowlands. Pico Duarte, at 3,175 m., which is also the highest point on all of the islands of the West Indies, is the highest elevation. The most important rivers of Hispaniola originate on Pico Duarte.

The very uneven distribution of rainfall shapes the vegetation of the islands. On the windward sides of the mountains there are evergreen rain and montane forests. The leeward slopes are covered with deciduous dry forests, which become wet and montane forests at higher elevations. The lowlands are also divided in two vegetation zones. The dry regions are covered with dry forest or take on savanna-like forms; the wet zones, which receive more precipitation, are carpeted with evergreen rain forest, provided they are not in agricultural use. Farming is the most important occupation in both Haiti and the Dominican Republic. With continual clearing, more and more areas fall victim to "modern times." At present, the island is still half-covered with forest, but increasing logging is proceeding ominously.

Hispaniolan Amazons are numerous on Hispaniola and are found in all environments. The daily routine of the

Hispaniolan Amazon, *Amazona ventralis*. Visible on this specimen are the blue primaries and white forehead and lores.

The wine-red belly patch is only suggested in these young Hispaniolan Amazons, *Amazona ventralis.* In the bird on the left, the black ear patch is not clearly defined.

Hispaniolan Amazon is very regular, as with virtually all amazon-parrot species. After sunrise, the parrots leave the roosting trees in very small flocks, mostly two to three birds, and set out with loud screeching in search of food. As soon as the birds have settled in the treetops, they become silent and are then no longer discernible in the foliage because of their coloration. An abundance of food is available to the Hispaniolan Amazons. They readily visit corn fields and fruit plantations and revel in the supply of seeds. In agricultural regions, the birds are hunted because of the damage they cause. Towards evening the birds fly back to their roosting trees. Often, 200–300 amazon parrots congregate on such trees.

The breeding season begins in March. In abandoned woodpecker holes or other tree cavities, two to four eggs, approximately 35.7 × 27.6 mm., are laid and incubated for about 25 days. As is true of all amazon-parrot species, the male birds do not take part in incubation. The only contribution of the cocks is feeding the hens. After a nestling period of approximately 52–60 days, the youngsters leave the nest, but are still cared for by the adult birds for a number of weeks.

In the western part of Puerto Rico, only isolated Hispaniolan Amazons are encountered today. In the 1960s, several hundred young amazons are said to have been brought into Puerto Rico. After no official certificate of health could be produced for the birds, they were released on the edge of the coastal zone. Many of the parrots were able to reach the interior and become naturalized. In San German, Puerto Rico, Bond (1971) was able to find two Hispaniolan Amazon nests. Apparently, today more Hispaniolan Amazons than Puerto Rican Amazons (*A. v. vittata*) are found on the island.

CARE AND BREEDING: On

Hispaniola, Hispaniolan Amazons are with great pleasure kept as cage birds by the natives. On Ascension Day, according to native belief, the youngsters are said to leave the nests. Many people search for young amazon parrots on this day in order to then sell them in local markets as pets.

Hispaniolan Amazons are quite rare in Europe. Two of them are currently exhibited in the Walsrode bird park (1980).

Apparently the first breeding succeeded in the Jersey zoo in 1971. Since 1964, the zoo had housed four

Distribution of *Amazona ventralis* on the island of Puerto Rico.

amazon parrots in its tropical bird house. Eggs were laid for the first time in 1968. The clutch was infertile, however. In April of 1969, three eggs were laid, of which one was fertile, but no young hatched. Only in 1971, after the amazon parrots had not been granted success for their efforts the year before either, did one chick hatch from a clutch of three eggs after an incubation period of approximately 26 days. The other two eggs were infertile. The female was fed regularly by the male during the incubation period, and came out of the nest box to feed herself again only when the youngster was about 35 days old. After

61 days in the nest, the young parrot left the tree trunk for a few minutes, and a week later it spent the night with the adult birds outside the nest. After 13 weeks of age, the youngster was completely self-sufficient.

A Swiss fancier named Fink was able to accomplish a successful breeding with Hispaniolan Amazons in 1979. In January of 1978 four birds were available. Two of the animals formed a pair, and the hen, after mating as well as feeding by the cock had taken place, laid the first four eggs in September of 1978. After 30 days, the eggs were removed because all were infertile. Since a change in location took place in the winter, it was April before the pair became interested in the nest box again. The pair kept in the adjoining flight no doubt had a stimulating effect.

From May 1st on, intensified mating attempts were observed. Four white eggs were laid on May 5, 7, 11, and 13, and were incubated continuously from the 7th of May on.

On June 1st, the first faint peeping was detected; the incubation period is therefore about 25–26 days. The second youngster hatched on the 2nd of June. The third hatched about the 7th of June. The fourth youngster was discovered in the inspection on June 10, after the adult birds were moved away for a short time. At an age of 8–10 days the grayish blue feather sheaths could be seen through the skin, while the younger birds are still pinkish flesh color. The egg tooth is still present. The feather sheaths began breaking through on the 15th day of life, and burst on the 20th day. The cries of the parents were answered on the 29th day. On the 30th day the wing and tail were a third their full length. The wing coverts had orange-colored edging, and the body feathers began to sprout. By the 40th day the young were almost completely feathered, flapped merrily,

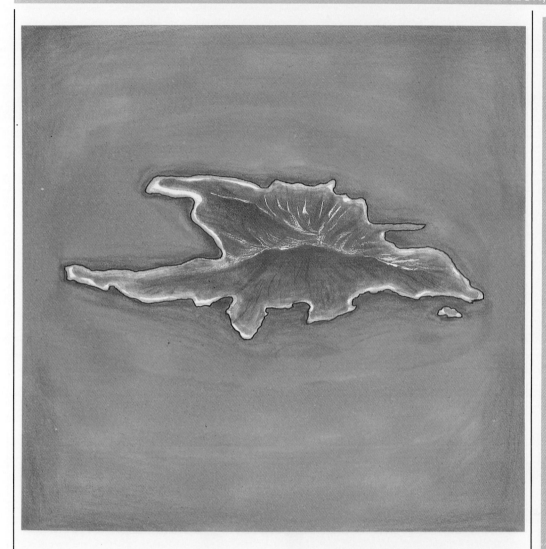

and looked out of the entrance hole from time to time. At 52 days, the first youngster came out of the box; the others followed almost according to the laying interval. Until the 10th of August, the young returned to the box for sleeping, and from this point in time also began to take food independently. By the 20th of August the young were virtually self-sufficient. They are somewhat duller in coloration. The forehead band, which is white in the adults, is almost yellow in the youngsters. The bills have black spots. The iris is still totally dark. Sex is recognizable by a difference in the coloration of the claws (?); female Hispaniolan Amazons have claws horn color to gray, while male birds have black claws. This character can already be seen in youngsters. After 16 youngsters had been reared (as of the spring of 1982), Fink is no longer completely certain that differently colored claws can be considered sexual characters.

Successful Hispaniolan Amazon broods are reported at the field station in the Luquillo Forest Preserve (El Yungue National Forest) in Puerto Rico.

In 1981 and 1982 a few Hispaniolan Amazons were imported into Germany, and so one has hope that a small breeding stock of this rare amazon parrot can be built up for the future.

Yellow-billed Amazon
Amazona collaria (Linnaeus) 1758

DESCRIPTION: Length approximately 28 cm.; green; under parts lighter green; lores, frontal band, and rear eye region white; upper part of head dark blue with black edging; stripe from bill to ear region blue, interspersed with white at bill; ear patch dark green-blue; broad wine-red stripe beginning on throat and neck, extending over cheeks, and ending below the occiput; nape feathers with dark edging; carpal edge blue; primaries blue; underside of wing blue green; tail feathers green, yellow green at the tip; outer tail feathers red at the base; orbital ring white; iris brown; bill yellowish horn color; feet grayish brown.

Youngsters: White on frontal band and lores barely present; only throat and front of neck wine red; iris dark brown.

RANGE: Central and eastern Jamaica.

Yellow-billed Amazon, *Amazona collaria*, in juvenile plumage; white on the frontal band and lores is only barely present, and only the throat and front of the neck are wine-red.

WAY OF LIFE: The island of Jamaica, which has been inhabited since the ninth century by the Arawaks Indians, was discovered in 1493 by Christopher Columbus. A mountain range traverses the island from west to east: it reaches elevations of almost 600 m. in the west; in the middle of the island, in the Central Range, elevations of about 950 m.; and in the east, an elevation of 2256 m. with the Blue Mountains Peak in the Blue Mountains. This mountain range intercepts the trade winds, producing diverse vegetation forms. The average annual precipitation amounts to over 2500 mm. in the north and under 1000 mm. in the south. The northern vegetation is tropical and forms an evergreen rain forest on the northern mountain slopes. In the southern part of the island dry savanna predominates. The coasts are edged with palms, and mangrove swamps readily form in the river estuaries.

Yellow-billed Amazons are resident in the eastern part of the island, in the John Crow Mountains; in the central portion, around Mount Diablo; as well as in the western part of the island, in the hilly Cockpit Country. The birds are forest dwellers but also fly to cultivated farm land in search of food. Outside of the breeding season small flocks the parrots, seldom of more than twenty birds and often together with Black-billed Amazons (*Amazona agilis*), travel through the forested regions in search of food. In the afternoon hours, the flight back to the habitual roosting sites takes place.

The breeding season begins in April. Two to four eggs, 36.0 × 29.2 mm., are said to be laid. The breeding cavities are reported to be located at great heights in old trees and palms. Young birds taken from the nest are offered in the markets in June and July.

CARE AND BREEDING: In the last

Yellow-billed Amazon, *Amazona collaria,* **a forest dweller native to the island of Jamaica. Conspicuous characteristics include a dark green-blue ear patch and a broad wine-red stripe beginning on the throat and neck.**

Top: Headstudy of a Yellow-billed Amazon, *Amazona collaria.* This species is only rarely found in the hands of even the most serious breeders. *Bottom:* Pair of Yellow-billed Amazons. A quick glance might suggest that the Yellow-billed Amazon resembles the juvenile Cuban Amazons.

century Yellow-billed Amazons were frequently imported into England and were offered at prices between fifteen and twenty shillings. In Germany these amazons are very rare; three Yellow-billed Amazons were to be found in the Walsrode bird park in 1980. They appeared to be very lively representatives of their species: constantly in motion, they also flew with great pleasure. Cursory examination might suggest that Yellow-billed Amazons resemble juveniles of the Cuban Amazon (*Amazona leucocephala*); in fact, they are considerably smaller than the Cuban.

The Keston Farm in England was able to report a hybrid breeding between a female Yellow-billed Amazon and a male Festive Amazon (*Amazona festiva*). The three young were raised by the adult birds and resembled the male in coloration, but were smaller than it.

In Ontario, Canada, four young Yellow-billed Amazons which had been taken from a nest in their homeland were raised by hand by a Mrs. Coltas in 1965. In 1972 or 1973 two young are said to have been raised by a Californian parrot fancier. Both youngsters were apparently deformed and died after a few years.

Ramon Noegel of the United States, who cares for a large amazon-parrot stock that includes very rare species and subspecies, was able to breed the Yellow-billed Amazon in 1982.

In 1981, several German bird importers brought this species into Germany, no doubt for the first time since the repeal of the parrot-importation ban. Most of the birds went into the care of experienced parrot breeders, and so one can entertain the hope that the first successful German breedings of *Amazona collaria* will soon be reported.

Puerto Rican Amazon

Amazona vittata (Boddaert) 1758 — only one remaining subspecies (the second is extinct).

1. *Amazona vittata vittata* (Boddaert)

DESCRIPTION: Length approximately 30 cm.; dark green, under parts somewhat lighter; all feathers of the upper parts, especially on the head and nape, have dark edging; lores and frontal band dark red; primaries and outer secondaries steel blue, blackish blue on the tips of the primaries; primary coverts and alula blue; underside of wing bluish green; tail feathers dark green with lighter green edging; outer tail feathers blue on the outer vane, red at the base of the inner vane; bill yellowish horn color; orbital ring white to brown; feet yellowish.

RANGE: Northeastern Puerto Rico.

2. *Amazona vittata gracilipes* (Ridgway)

DESCRIPTION: Smaller than the nominate form; feet also smaller.

RANGE: The island of Culebra (east of Puerto Rico); possibly the island of Vieques (about 20 km. south of Culebra).

REMARKS: The Culebran subspecies of the Puerto Rican Amazon must have become extinct in the period between 1900–1912. In 1899 it was still common on the 28 sq. km. island. In 1912 it was searched for in vain. In 1927 it was reported to Wetmore that on the island of Vieques parrots had once been observed there in the dense forests of the southern part of the island. If Puerto Rican Amazons ever did occur on Vieques, then they must have become extinct there around the turn of the century as well. Three specimens of *Amazona vittata gracilipes* can be found in the National Museum in Washington, DC.

WAY OF LIFE: The island of Puerto Rico, which was discovered in 1493 by Columbus on his second voyage, served in past centuries as a rich source of wood. Around the turn of the last century, the logging reached its peak and began to decline. Today, Puerto Rico is the most densely populated island of the Greater Antilles (350 inhabitants per sq. km.) and has evolved from an agricultural to an industrial country. The range of the Puerto Rican Amazon became more and more restricted as a result of the century-long deforestation. Today, only the Luquillo montane-forest reserve (approximately 44 square miles) serves as a last refuge for the remaining amazon parrots. Situated in the northeastern part of Puerto Rico, it has a maximum elevation of 1,065 m. and consists of tropical rain forest to an elevation of 400 m. and beyond that an evergreen montane forest with very dense stands of the sierra palm. The census which was carried out from August 1953 to March 1956 in the Luquillo National Forest Reserve showed a population of only about 200 birds—probably the entire stock of the Puerto Rican Amazon. Recher and Recher saw only 15 birds in 1966 but estimated a maximum of 50 animals. In 1968, Dr. C. Kepler determined that only about 20 amazon parrots still existed. In 1971 the population decreased to about 15 birds, and in 1975 only 13 remained. With these statistics it must be remembered that the one hundred percent of the population was not included, since the censuses always took place in the spring, when the birds have sought out their ancestral breeding sites. Juveniles (sexual maturity may be expected to occur only in the fifth or sixth year of life) could not be counted completely. On the basis of the alarming decline of

the amazon-parrot population, a program to protect and ensure the survival of the remaining Puerto Rican Amazons was put into action by the U.S. Fish and Wildlife Service in the El Yungue National Forest Reserve. Thus a number of amazon parrots are kept at the Luquillo field station for breeding purposes; however, most of the birds are females. At the same time, the breeding pairs in the wild are monitored from the field station. A worker from the field station takes the eggs from the nests and places plaster-of-paris eggs under the incubating amazon parrots. The eggs are then placed in an incubator and subsequently returned to the breeding pair as nestlings, so that losses do not occur during incubation. Very lamentable is the fact that the nestlings are afflicted by larvae of the bot fly.

One young amazon parrot taken from the nest was infested with hundreds of these maggots, but could still be saved with intensive treatment. Studies showed that almost 20% of all youngsters were attacked by maggots.

Other natural enemies of the amazon parrots are the Red-tailed Hawk (*Buteo jamaicensis*) and the Broad-winged Hawk (*Buteo platypterus*) which kill even adult birds. Rodriquez-Vidal concluded in 1956 that four of six nests had been destroyed by rats (*Rattus rattus*). A very great threat comes from the Pearly-eyed Thrasher (*Margarops fuscatus*), which as a cavity breeder competes with the parrots for breeding sites and also destroys occupied parrot nests and eats the eggs. Thrasher numbers continue to increase. Since the amazon parrots also require rather large nest cavities, the supply of

The Puerto Rican Amazon, *Amazona vittata vittata*, is the only remaining subspecies of *A. vittata*, *A. v. gracilipes* being extinct. The range of *A. v. vittata* is restricted to northeastern Puerto Rico, but the race is granted protection under the law.

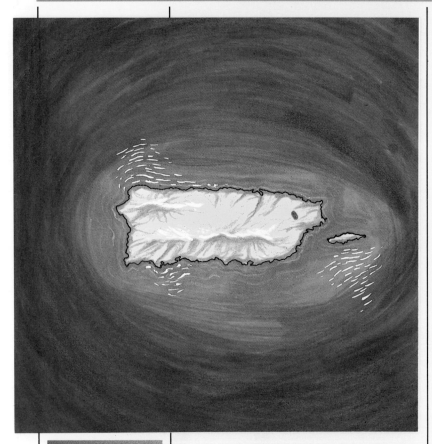

Distribution of *Amazona vittata* on the island of Puerto Rico.

to two hours, and then fly, always along the same route, around the surrounding mountain peaks. Flight over the higher peaks has not been observed; apparently, the higher regions are avoided because of the usually low-hanging blanket of clouds. The feeding trees (among others, *Dacryodes excelsa*), which for the most part are located at a distance of one km. from the roosting trees, are typically visited until they have been depleted. The preferred food is the fruit of the sierra palm (*Euterpe globosa*), which bears fruit from November to June. The flight back to the roosting trees takes place by the same route as the flight out. Rodriques-Vidal established that Puerto Rican Amazons feed on more than 50 different fruits. Dr. C. Kepler points out the possibility that some essential nutrient is not available in the refuge, and the amazon parrots are therefore forced to leave the refuge in the summer months.

According to Dr. C. Kepler, the breeding season extends from February to June, during the dry season. The breeding cavities are located 6–15 m. above the ground. In the Luquillo Forest Reserve all nests found were in palo colorado trees (*Cyrilla racemiflora*). Dr. Kepler found a nest in 1970 that contained two eggs on March 15 and three eggs on March 23. On the 5th of April the first chick hatched. On May 27, all three youngsters were already fledged, and two days later he saw the family group flying three km. from the nest. An examination of 19 amazon parrot nests in the years 1953–1969 indicated that from 40 eggs laid, 18 youngsters left the nest. In the three breeding seasons of the years 1969–71, four out of five nests were unsuccessful.

CARE AND BREEDING: It appears that two Puerto Rican Amazons were kept in the London Zoo around the turn of

available nest sites is decreasing. Many tree cavities are often under water because of the continual rainfall and therefore cannot be used. The workers at the field station have enlarged existing natural cavities and have also drilled holes in the floor so that any water entering can immediately drain out.

It can only be hoped that the measures undertaken will give the remaining amazon parrots a real chance. Only the future will tell if the extant existing stock of about 15 birds are sufficient to ensure survival of the species.

In the wild, the life of the amazons follows a predictable daily routine. The nesting and roosting trees are located in the "La Mina" region at about 650 m. above sea level. At daybreak, the amazon parrots make a racket for one the century. Perhaps these amazons were marketed more often before 1900, when their populations were larger, but were not recognized as Puerto Rican Amazons, as the great similarity to the smaller Black-billed Amazon (*Amazona agilis*) could lead to confusion. The Patuxent Research Center in Maryland has three birds in captivity for breeding purposes.

Puerto Rican Amazons are of course listed in Appendix I of the Washington Convention (CITES).

Black-billed Amazon
Amazona agilis (Linnaeus) 1758

DESCRIPTION: Length approximately 25 cm.; dark green; upper part of head dark bluish green; red feathers on the forehead; neck feathers have dark edging; trace of a dark ear patch; primaries and secondaries dark blue; secondaries green toward base; small red speculum, absent in the female; underside of wing blue green; tail green; outer tail feathers blue, yellow green with red spot on the inner vane toward the base; iris dark brown; orbital ring dark gray; bill dark gray; feet dark gray.

RANGE: Interior of the island of Jamaica.

WAY OF LIFE: The island of Jamaica, which belongs to the Greater Antilles, is the homeland of the Black-billed Amazon. With an area of 10,962 sq. km. and 192 inhabitants per sq. km., Jamaica is relatively densely populated and has evolved from an agricultural to an industrial nation since the Second World War. Tourism has also increased substantially. In the interior of the country, cattle breeding occupies a wide area, which can of course lead to a conversion of scrubland and forest into grassland. Recently the government has

concerned itself with extending the small forested regions that still exist.

Black-billed Amazons primarily occur in the wet forests surrounding Mount Diablo in the interior of the country, as well as the adjoining Cockpit Country to the west. In the John Crow Mountains (the eastern part of the Blue Mountains), Black-billed Amazons have no longer been sighted, although they were still common in this region in the last century.

Outside of the breeding season, Black-billed Amazons form small foraging flocks, together with the other amazon-parrot species that occurs on Jamaica, the Yellow-billed Amazon. They attract attention to themselves only during flight, when they make the typical amazon-parrot clamor, which, by the way, is similar to that of the Yellow-billed Amazon. When feeding

Male Black-billed Amazon, *Amazona agilis*. The species *A. agilis* is the smallest member of its genus.

Distribution of *Amazona agilis* on the island of Jamaica. The author questions the easternmost proposed distribution.

in the tall trees and palms, the birds are very quiet and are barely detectable in the foliage of the trees thanks to their uniform green coloration.

Of the breeding habits it is known only that beginning in April they incubate two to four eggs in highly situated tree cavities.

It appears, based on the paucity of observations and records, that the population of Black-billed Amazons is decreasing and can be maintained at the present level only by means of statutory measures.

CARE AND BREEDING: The Black-billed Amazon, one of the smallest species of its genus, was once again imported into Germany in 1981. Before that, only isolated specimens had been kept by fanciers. Although the population of the Black-billed Amazon has been decimated in recent years, the Jamaican government has decided to allow a limited number of the birds to be captured and exported, especially since they are considered pests by most of the native population. Thus approximately 400 parrots were exported to the United States and Canada in 1978. The exportations to central Europe, and Germany in particular, took place later.

Black-billed Amazons in the main do not differ in their behavior from other small amazon-parrot species. H. Leibfahrt informed the author that his Black-billed Amazons, kept in a flock in an outdoor flight, had developed into very loud screechers after the acclimation period; they often produce their shrill calls for hours on end for no apparent reason.

No breeding successes with the Black-billed Amazon are known from Europe. In 1979, a youngster is said to have hatched in the aviaries of R. Noegel in Florida. Unfortunately, no further details are available.

Red-necked Amazon
Amazona arausiaca (P. L. S. Müller) 1766

DESCRIPTION: Length approximately 40 cm.; green; feathers on the upper parts have dark edging; head blue, changing into green on the cheeks and occiput; throat red, which may extend as far as the breast; primaries green, becoming blue toward tip; secondaries green, the three outer feathers showing a red speculum; tail feathers green, yellow green toward tip, the outer feathers red on the inner vane toward base; iris orange; orbital ring whitish; bill light horn gray, darker toward tip; feet gray brown. Females are said to be much larger (?).

Youngsters: Blue on head not as extensive (?); red throat patch smaller (?); iris dark brown.

RANGE: Dominica, West Indies.

WAY OF LIFE: Dominica, the northernmost of the Windward Islands, which are part of the Lesser Antilles, is home to the Red-necked Amazon. With an area of 751 sq. km., Dominica is about the size of New York City; however, with approximately 75,000 inhabitants, of which 10,000 live in the capital of Roseau, it is relatively sparsely populated. Like the other islands of the Lesser Antilles, Dominica was created by volcanic action. In the north-south direction, the island is traversed by a very rugged mountain range. The highest elevation, 1447 m., is attained by the Morne Diablotin. The interior of the island is covered with dense tropical rain forest; penetration seems to be virtually impossible. Low-hanging rain clouds allow the extremely high humidity to reach almost 100%. In addition, the high temperatures (average annual temperature about 28°C) promote the growth of vegetation. In the lowlands, more and more woodland is being cleared for cultivation, in order to grow citrus fruits, bananas, cocoa, and spices. The habitat of Red-necked Amazon is becoming ever more limited, and the flocks diminish in size. The native population's passion for hunting represents a serious threat to survival; they shoot at anything that moves. In a German travel brochure, in which, among other things, the sporting activities on Dominica are listed, bird hunting is included, just like riding or tennis.

Red-necked Amazon, *Amazona arausiaca*, a very attractive and very threatened parrot of Dominica, West Indies.

This Red-necked Amazon, *Amazona arausiaca*, has a less-defined red throat patch than is characteristic for its species. This less-defined patch is not a sex character.

Red-necked Amazons live principally in the forest regions located in the southeastern part of the island and on the slopes of Morne Diablotin. The amazon parrots favor the low-lying forest zones and are seldom encountered at elevations above 600 m. Although the Red-necked Amazon and its distribution have long been known, little is recorded about its life history and breeding habits.

It is very interesting that two amazon-parrot species evolved in the small environment of Jamaica. The second amazon species that occurs on the island is the still rarer Imperial Amazon (*Amazona imperialis*), which inhabits the forests located at higher elevations.

Karl Neunzig (1920) reported that the Red-necked Amazon occurred throughout the island and were frequently seen in large flocks. Thereafter, the number of birds was to steadily decrease. It is almost unbelievable how man can change,

disrupt, or destroy in a short period of time what has taken millennia to evolve.

Great damage to the population also results from the hurricanes that occur yearly. Not only are birds injured or killed during such storms, but, much more significantly, the storms do heavy damage to the trees. Many of the trees that are used by the amazon parrots for feeding and nesting are destroyed.

A few years ago, the author was able to visit the island of Dominica for a short time. He was informed by a native that an American tourist had offered $4,000 (at the time about 10,000 DM) for a pair of Red-necked Amazons. In any case, the American's stay was cut short, and the "deal" did not take place. The ramifications of an offer of this kind are apparently understood by very few people. To be sure, at first glance one sees this merely as $4,000 for two amazon parrots, but the consequence is that news of the lucrative possibilities in trading birds will spread in no time, and without doubt every other family will launch its own trapping expedition. In no time at all this island population will be condemned to extinction.

During the author's stay on Dominica, in the southeastern part of the island, he observed three parrots in flight in the late afternoon. Because of the great distance, however, it could not be determined whether they were Red-necked or Imperial amazons, or a mixture of both.

CARE AND BREEDING: Around the turn of the century a few Red-necked Amazons reached Europe. On Dominica, in 1930, the Englishman Sydney Porter obtained one male and two female Red-necked Amazons, which had been shot and therefore were badly injured. On the ocean voyage to Europe, one of the females died; the second died a short time later in England. The remaining bird was

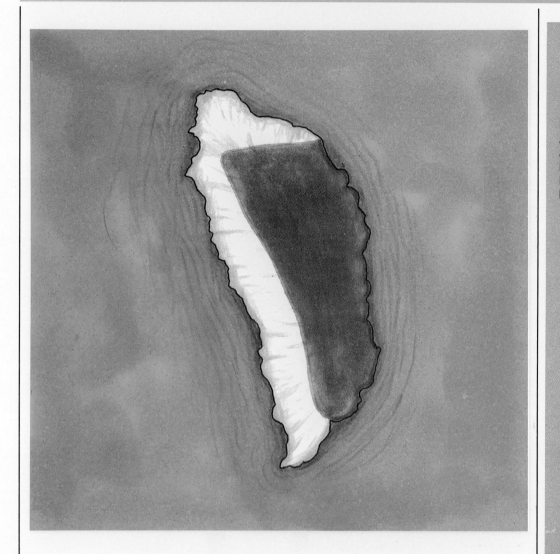

Distribution of *Amazona arausiaca* on the island of Dominica, West Indies.

extremely tame, playful, and charming. Porter described it as the most intelligent of all parrots.

The zoo on the island Jersey (north of France) keeps one male and two female Red-necked Amazons. Two Red-necked Amazons can be seen in the Walsrode bird park (1980). Those exhibited in Walsrode may be the only parrots of this species in Germany. It cannot be expected that this amazon-parrot species can ever again be kept by private fanciers.

D. Green succeeded in crossing a Red-necked Amazon with a Yellow-crowned Amazon (*A. ochrocephala ochrocephala* or *A. o. panamensis*) in 1970 on Dominica. This hybrid was very similar in appearance to the Red-necked Amazon, but the yellow forehead was contributed by the Yellow-crowned Amazon. The youngster, of course, was fertile—a further demonstration of the particularly close relationships among *Amazona* species—and was mated with a Red-necked Amazon in 1977. The hybrid was virtually a pure-bred Red-necked Amazon in appearance; only the few yellow feathers on the forehead pointed to the other amazon species.

The Red-necked Amazon is listed in Appendix I of the Washington Convention (CITES).

St. Lucia Amazon

Amazona versicolor (P. L. S. Müller) 1776

DESCRIPTION: Length approximately 43 cm.; green; feathers heavily edged, particularly on the upper parts; forehead, frontal band, and lores violet blue, changing into lighter blue in the occiput, eye region, and the cheeks; red band running over the throat; breast and belly wine red, feathers often spotted with green; lower belly, rump, and thighs green; carpal edge yellow green; red speculum on the three outer primaries; primaries and secondaries green, blue towards tip; underside of wing bluish green; tail feathers green, yellow at the tip; outer tail feathers with red and blue spot at the base; iris orange; orbital ring grayish brown; bill grayish brown; feet dark gray.

Youngsters: Brown iris.

RANGE: Saint Lucia, West Indies.

WAY OF LIFE: The St. Lucia Amazon, the second largest of all amazon parrots, is found on the Caribbean island of Saint Lucia. Saint Lucia, with an area of 616 sq. km., is home to 115,000 people, 45,000 of which live in the capital of Castries. With a constant temperature throughout the year of about 28°C on a monthly average, the northeastern trade winds determine the annual rainfall. The southwest receives about 1,200 mm. of rainfall, and the mountains of the northeast receive about 3,000 mm. annually. The Morne Gimie (950 m.) and the two Pitons (elevation about 800 m.) located in the southwest are the principal features of the island. The final refuge of the St. Lucia Amazon is in the vicinity of the Morne Gimie, on the eastern and northern slopes, delimited in the north by the headwaters of the Cul de Sac and extending south as far as the Barre de l'Isle Ridge. The area occupied by

the amazon parrots now amounts to only 50 sq. km. In 1975, the remaining population in this region was estimated at about 100–200 birds. The St. Lucia Amazon, next to the Puerto Rican Amazon (*Amazona vittata vittata*), is the most threatened species of its genus.

Outside the breeding season the parrots assemble in small flocks of up to twelve animals. The birds spend the night in the higher mountain regions. In the early morning they fly with a great clamor to their feeding trees. They spend the entire day diligently searching for food; in the course of feeding they seldom fly above the treetops, so they are very difficult to recognize. The parrots like to feed on fleshy fruits from, for example, *Licania macrophylla* and *L. membranacea*. Palm fruits are also taken readily. The animals apparently do not enter cultivated land.

The breeding season is said to begin in March or April. Data concerning breeding and nesting habits could not be obtained by the author. The incubation period probably amounts to 25–26 days, as in other amazon-parrot species. The nestling period of the youngsters can last 70 to 80 days (?).

The greatest danger to the amazon parrots comes from hunting. Despite the legislative ban, the annual loss from shooting is estimated to be about 40 birds. With a population of at most 200 animals, the present shooting quota is a threat to the survival of the St. Lucia Amazon. It is to be hoped that the forestry officials of St. Lucia will succeed in putting an end to the poaching.

Hurricane Allen, which struck the island on August 4 and 5, 1980, and in many areas caused catastrophic damage to property, was not equally devastating in all parts of the island. The area occupied by the St. Lucia Amazon is said to have been spared the worst damage. Other sources, however, describe the destruction of nesting and feeding trees and voice the fear that the St. Lucia Amazon will soon be added to the list of extinct species.

The St. Lucia Naturalist's Society is at the moment very intensively working for the survival of this species (K. L. Schuchmann). Much as with the doomed-to-extinction Puerto Rican Amazon (*Amazona vittata vittata*), artificial nest cavities are placed in the breeding localities of the St. Lucia Amazon, thus providing additional nesting opportunities. The Pearly-eyed Thrasher (*Margarops fuscatus*) not only competes with the amazon parrots for nesting sites on Puerto Rico but also succeeds in taking the nesting sites of the much larger St. Lucia Amazon. But the thrasher cannot use the artificial nesting cavities because of the depth of 1.6 m. According to Schuchmann, St. Lucia Amazons have already been observed cautiously examining the artificial nests.

It is of course open to question whether the measures instituted in 1981 will contribute to the survival of the amazons. These emergency measures were probably introduced much too late, and it is feared that the species will be extinct before the end of the century.

CARE AND BREEDING: The St. Lucia Amazons were already endangered in the last century and could only very rarely be obtained for zoos. In 1874 and 1875 they reached the zoo in London. The Duke of Bedford obtained a St. Lucia Amazon which had been captured on St. Lucia in 1950. The East Winds Inn on St. Lucia had a St. Lucia Amazon in the hotel aviary in 1975. Apparently, this amazon parrot has never been kept in Germany.

In the Wildlife Preservation Trust on the island of Jersey, one of the Channel Islands off the north coast of France, there are nine St. Lucia Amazons.

Seven of these birds reached Jersey with a special permit issued by the government of St. Lucia that provided for a breeding program that might help to preserve these extremely endangered birds. Here the amazon parrots are kept in pairs in large flights. The ninth amazon parrot was kept by itself. Unfortunately, no endoscopic examinations were done, so that there is no guarantee as to the sexes. It is believed, however, that there are four pairs because the animals get along very well. Since the birds reached the zoo as youngsters, one can hope that the first breeding attempts will soon occur. It will become evident whether the pairs were placed together correctly or incorrectly.

The director of the bird department of the Jersey zoo, David Jeggo, informed G. Mühlhaus (1980) that two females had already laid eggs, which unfortunately were infertile.

The second largest amazon parrot, the Saint Lucia Amazon, *Amazona versicolor*, often exhibits variable coloration of the breast and belly plumage. On the bird perched on the left, the red breast band is well defined.

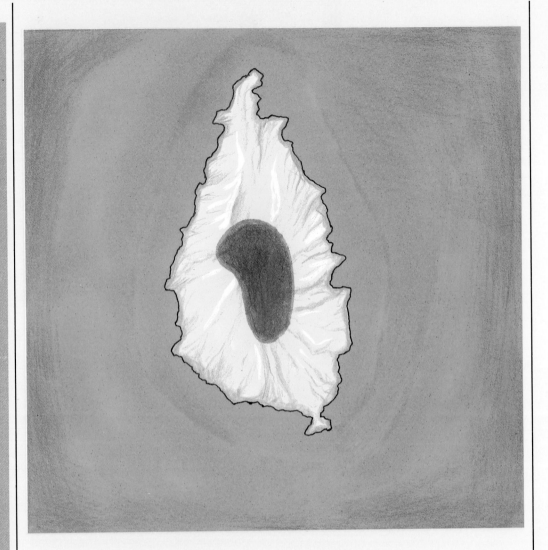

Distribution of *Amazona versicolor* on the island of Saint Lucia, West Indies.

The St. Lucia Amazons on Jersey exhibit quite variable coloration on the breast and belly plumage. In several birds the red patch on the throat is barely visible, while in others this marking is prominent. No change in plumage coloration has been observed in the course of the five years; thus it remains to be seen whether the birds without the red throat patch will change in the future.

It is to be hoped that the Jersey Zoo will succeed in breeding the St. Lucia Amazons in the coming years. The survival of this rare amazon-parrot species in captivity at least would then be guaranteed.

Jacobsen informed the author of a supposedly successful breeding on Bermuda in 1968. A married couple kept a pair of St. Lucia Amazons in a small flight which was furnished to resemble a rain-forest landscape. It must be assumed from the very meager data that the eggs were laid at intervals of two days. After an incubation period of 28 days, the chicks hatched in the same sequence and interval in which the eggs were laid. The chicks were then raised by the adults without complications.

The St. Lucia Amazon is listed in Appendix I of the Washington Convention (CITES).

Violet Amazon
Amazona violacea (Gmelin) 1788

REMARKS: Already extinct in the eighteenth century. *Psittacus violaceus* Gmelin, Syst. Nat., 1, pt. 1788, p. 337 ("Insulae aquarum Lupiarum")—in describing the Violet Amazon, Gmelin relied on the unconfirmed statements of explorers. In fact, occurrence of an amazon-parrot species on Guadeloupe has yet to be proved, but it can nevertheless be assumed that Gmelin's thesis is correct. It is conceivable that the amazon parrots living on Guadeloupe became extinct through natural catastrophes, such as through hurricanes and eruptions of the presently still active volcano Soufrière.

Martinique Amazon
Amazona martinica Clark 1905

REMARKS: It is assumed that an amazon-parrot species (or subspecies) occurred on the island of Martinique in the Lesser Antilles.

Dominica, about 50 km. north, and St. Lucia, about 50 km. south of Martinique, which exhibit virtually the same terrain and vegetation, are inhabited by amazon parrots (*A. arausiaca, A. versicolor, A. imperialis,* and *A. guildingii*) today.

Amazona martinicana Clark, *Auk,* 22 (1905), p. 343 (Martinique)—Clark described the Martinique Amazon in 1905 after it had already been extinct for over 100 years. On the basis of old travelers' reports and ships' logs it is completely credible that amazon parrots occurred on Martinique. Whether the parrots were brought to the island by Caribbean Indians or were an independent wild population can no longer be determined today.

The author suspects that all of the islands of the Lesser Antilles including Barbados were inhabited by amazon parrots in previous centuries. Unfortunately, this theory cannot be substantiated.

This rare Imperial Amazon, *Amazona imperialis,* photographed in the Walsrode bird park, is the only representative of its species in Germany.

The largest member of the genus *Amazona*, the Imperial Amazon, *A. imperialis*, reaches a length of approximately 46 cm. Because these impressive birds prefer the higher mountain regions, their existence is less immediately threatened than that of many other amazon parrot species.

Imperial Amazon
Amazona imperialis (Richmond) 1899

DESCRIPTION: Length approximately 46 cm.; upper parts green; crown of head, eye and ear regions violet, edged with dark turquoise; frontal band, lores, cheeks, neck, throat, breast, belly edged with wine-red violet; carpal edge and speculum red; primaries dark blue, green at the base; secondaries green, violet blue at the tip; underside of wing green; tail feathers dark red-brown, edged; under tail coverts, rump, and thigh green; iris orange red; orbital ring dark gray; bill dark horn-gray; feet dark gray.

Youngsters: Occiput and nape green; rear part of cheeks greenish; iris dark brown.

RANGE: Dominica, West Indies.

WAY OF LIFE: The largest member of genus *Amazona*, the Imperial Amazon, is, along with the Red-necked Amazon (*Amazona arausiaca*), indigenous to the island of Dominica in the Lesser Antilles. Imperial Amazons dwell mainly in the higher mountain regions and therefore are threatened only to a limited extent.

The mountainous regions of Dominica are still for the most part unexplored, and the dense rain forests provide the parrots with an abundant food supply. While feeding or during other activities in the treetops, the amazons' lustrous plumage offers excellent protection. Only during flight, when they screech and whistle shrilly, can they be detected.

A powerful hurricane that struck the island of Dominica in 1928 drove nearly 200 amazon parrots into the settled coastal regions. According to Sydney Porter (1929) at least 38 amazon parrots from this flock were shot. Fortunately, the birds withdrew into the inaccessible mountains a short time later.

It appears that the Imperial Amazons today live only in pairs or in family groups. One seldom sees larger flocks or associations with Red-necked Amazons. After sunrise and before the fall of darkness their loud screeches are sounded; they are silent during the day. Nothing is known about the breeding habits except that the nest cavities are located high up in the trees and that only two eggs (45.6 × 37.3 mm.) are laid.

CARE AND BREEDING: The Imperial Amazon is listed in Appendix I of the Washington Convention (CITES) and may not be traded. One of these

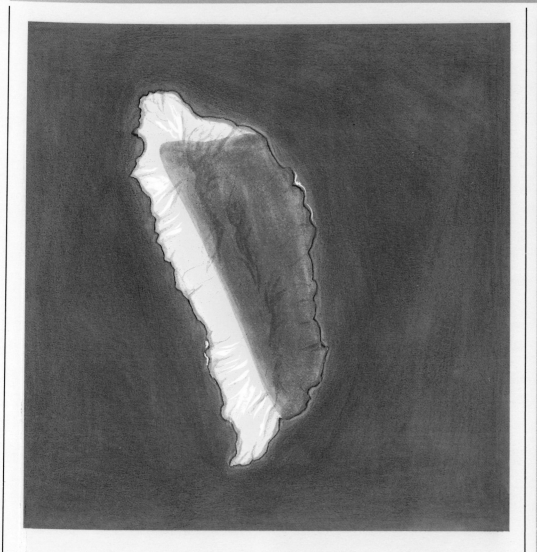

Distribution of *Amazona imperialis* on the island of Dominica, West Indies.

magnificent amazon parrots is found in the collection of the Walsrode bird park (1980). A Yellow-faced Amazon (*Amazona xanthops*), having a length of about 27 cm. and which is exhibited in the same aviary, emphasizes the imposing appearance of the Imperial Amazon even more. Unfortunately, the author was only able to observe this beautifully colored amazon parrot during the midday hours; the bird proved to be very sleepy at this time. Thus no conclusions about the bird's habits could be drawn from this encounter. It is known that virtually all parrot species retire at noon and take a short "midday nap."

The amazon parrot kept at Walsrode is apparently the first to reach Germany. In the London Zoo, Imperial Amazons were exhibited in 1865, 1901, and 1961.

S. Porter was able to nurse an injured Imperial Amazon back to health on Dominica in 1928. After the initial difficulties, the bird developed into an amiable, devoted pet and made friends with Porter's two Red-necked Amazons.

With this extremely endangered Caribal amazon parrot in particular, one must ask whether these animals still have any chance at all of surviving in their present environment. To be sure, nature reserves offer the birds a safe refuge, but only time will tell whether this single measure will ensure the survival of the species.

St. Vincent Amazon
Amazona guildingii (Vigors) 1836

DESCRIPTION: Length approximately 40 cm.; lustrous green, olive, and brownish; feathers with dark edging; crown, forehead, lores, and eye region whitish yellow; cheeks, occiput, throat yellow, becoming orange toward body; blue patch behind eye; breast and belly bronze; bend of wing olive green; carpal edge orange; outer primaries green, becoming violet toward tip; inner primaries green; outer secondaries violet blue; inner secondaries green, violet blue toward tip; primaries and secondaries orange and violet-blue at the base; greater wing coverts orange brown, green at the base; median and lesser wing coverts bronze, edged with greenish and bluish; underside of wing yellow; tail feathers orange at the base, abutting a wide band of violet blue, at the tip light orange yellow; iris orange; orbital ring gray; bill light yellowish; feet gray.

Youngsters: Breast, belly, rump, and under tail coverts olive green; underside of wing green; iris brown.

The coloration of the St. Vincent Amazon can be very rich in variation. There are some amazon parrots that differ considerably from the previous description. In the wild several specimens have been sighted that exhibited a complete or partial black coloration. Black coloration (melanism) can occur temporarily or permanently, whereby melanin, a brownish black water-insoluble substance of animal or plant origin (for example, from tyrosine), acts as the pigment responsible for the dark coloration of the feathers.

RANGE: St. Vincent, West Indies.

REMARKS: N. A. Vigors named the St. Vincent Amazon in honor of the naturalist and painter Lansdown Guilding (1797–1831), who was born in Kingstown, St. Vincent: *Psittacus Guildingii* 1836 (1837).

WAY OF LIFE: St. Vincent, a volcanic island of the Lesser Antilles, is the homeland of the stately St. Vincent Amazon. The 345 sq. km. island, presumably discovered by Columbus but only settled in the eighteenth century, is inhabited by about 100,000 people. The production of arrowroot gives the island a monopoly on the world market. Agriculture stamps the island's appearance. More and more tracts of forest give way to new farm land. The north-to-south mountain range with the Richmond Peak (1,074 m.) and the Soufrière (1,234 m.) still appears to be relatively undisturbed. The humid tropical climate with an average temperature of 28°C promotes vegetative growth. From June to December the northern trade winds bring precipitation of approximately 1,200 mm. in the coastal region and up to 3,800 mm. in the mountains. The months from January to May are free of precipitation.

Saint Vincent Amazon, *Amazona guildingii*. The quickly vanishing tropical uplands of the small Caribbean island of Saint Vincent serve as the last refuge for this rare, endangered amazon parrot.

St. Vincent Amazons live in the tropical mountain forests. Particularly in the northern part of the island, on the slopes and in the valleys of the Soufrière, they are still found in rather large numbers. The gregarious birds, like all other species of their genus, lead a regular life. Outside the breeding season, groups of 20 to 30 parrots assemble in order to search for food together. Once the feeding trees are reached, they are relinquished only very reluctantly. If danger threatens, the small parrot flock flies away but returns to the feeding site a short time later. The birds readily visit farm land in order to feed on cultivated fruits. The parrots stay primarily in the tropical rain forest, which is fully developed with large treetops on the lower and intermediate mountain slopes. The higher mountain regions with low-growing forest are not used by the parrots.

The breeding season of the St. Vincent Amazon begins sometime in April, shortly before the end of the dry season. Because of the large size of these amazon parrots, only large trees can offer adequate nesting facilities. Apparently only two eggs are laid. The nestling period of the youngsters coincides with the start of the rainy season. No doubt many clutches and youngsters fall victim to the water that is trapped in the nest cavities. Examination of the nest sites of the Puerto Rican Amazon (*Amazona vittata vittata*) showed that the tree cavities used by the parrots often were flooded, and the eggs therefore rotted. A similar situation must apply to the clutches and youngsters of the St. Vincent Amazon. Other cavity-nesting bird species must also be affected by this natural phenomenon; as long as a viable population of animals exists, however, this natural regulation is allowable. In the case of the St. Vincent Amazons, however, other

unfavorable factors that further reduce the birds' chances of survival are also at work: (1) hurricanes that appear annually in August and September; (2) conversion of the environment into agricultural land; (3) felling trees for lumber; (4) hunting the birds for food; (5) hunting the birds for "sport"; (6) robbing nests in order to sell the youngsters. If one wants to save the remaining population of St. Vincent Amazons, which is estimated at a few hundred animals, then measures that would counter the above-mentioned factors should be introduced. It simply makes no sense to list the animals in Appendix I of the Washington Convention (CITES) when destruction of the needed environment continues at the same time.

CARE AND BREEDING: The extremely rare St. Vincent Amazons are probably no longer to be found in the aviaries of

Saint Vincent Amazon, *Amazona guildingii*. The wild numbers of this very attractive parrot are estimated to be in the low hundreds. If the Saint Vincent Amazon is to be saved from extinction, man must take immediate action.

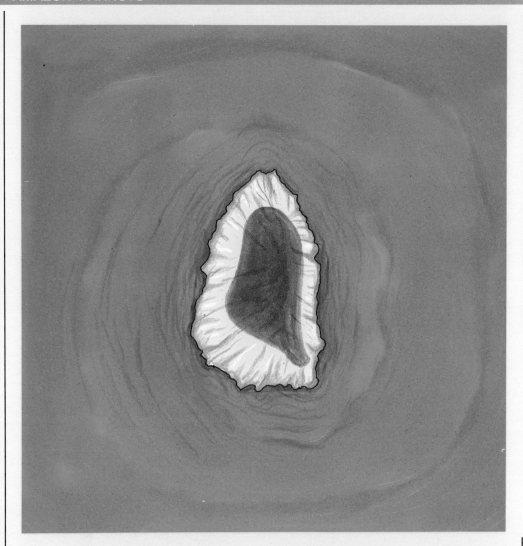

Distribution of *Amazona guildingii* on the island of Saint Vincent, West Indies.

bird fanciers. In Germany, one can admire three St. Vincent Amazons in the collection of the Walsrode bird park (1980). The park administration hopes for a successful breeding.

In 1971, the Brookfield Zoo delivered the St. Vincent Amazon that had been in their possession to Houston, Texas, where a second specimen was located. Already in 1972 the successful rearing of a youngster was achieved. An egg was laid on both March 28 and April 1. The female started incubating after laying the second egg. The youngster hatched on the 25th of April (incubation period, 25 days). The second egg was infertile and was removed. The young amazon

parrot opened its eyes after about 14 days. From then on the male bird participated in the feeding. By 67 days the youngster had left the nest cavity, but the adults still continued to feed it.

Miller, of Barbados, West Indies, keeps several St. Vincent Amazons and has been able to successfully breed these animals often in past years. The majority of the youngsters are said to have been shipped to the United States.

Although a direct threat to survival of the St. Vincent Amazon does not yet exist, a steady decline in the population has been observed, so every effort needs to be made in order to save this species.

Yellow-faced Amazon
Amazona xanthops (Spix) 1824

DESCRIPTION: Length approximately 27 cm.; green; head, nape, chin, throat yellow; yellow nape often interspersed with dark green feathers; ear region more yellow orange; upper belly red orange; thigh light green; carpal edge yellow green; primaries and secondaries green, blue green on the outer vane; secondary and primarily wing coverts green, edged with yellow; tail feathers green, yellow green toward tip; outer tail feathers red on the inner vane toward base; iris yellow orange; orbital ring white; bill light horn color, ridge of upper mandible grayish; feet gray.

Youngsters: The yellow feather areas are very limited; breast and belly green, interspersed with a few yellow feathers; iris brown. The change in coloration takes several years.

RANGE: Eastern and central Brazil from southern Piauí to São Paulo, Goias, and Mato Grosso.

WAY OF LIFE: There is only meager information on the Yellow-faced Amazon in the wild. The often very inaccessible terrain makes tracking down and observing this rare amazon-parrot species difficult. Prof. Dr. H. Sick reports that the birds are inhabitants of vegetation typical of the landforms, which is to say that they inhabit open mixed deciduous woodlands. In the Mato Grosso,

Distribution of
Amazona xanthops.

Yellow-faced Amazon, *Amazona xanthops.* In this fully colored individual the continuous breast band exhibited by some specimens is not present.

Presumably, this Red-lored Amazon, *Amazona autumnalis autumnalis*, is a female, as indicated by the flat shape of the head and the yellow coloring in the cheek feathers.

Yellow-faced Amazons are occasionally found in the savanna-like regions that are interspersed with bushes and trees. No reports exist concerning their breeding habits. According to Schönwetter (1964) the elliptical eggs are 40.5 × 31.9 mm.

CARE AND BREEDING: Dr. K. Russ reports that two Yellow-faced Amazons were imported by Hagenbeck in 1879 for a bird exhibition in Berlin. In the collection of the Walsrode bird park there is a Yellow-faced Amazon, which, judging from its coloration, must only be a few years old. The possibility certainly exists that the extent of the yellow areas of plumage on the head, breast, and belly can vary considerably, and that the amount of yellow is not an indicator of age.

Johann Natterer (1781–1843), who lived in Brazil for a number of years, described the Yellow-faced Amazon as a "stupid" bird. Statements of this kind should not be applied to a species as a whole, especially as the statement was made at a time when a parrot was supposed to be tame after a few days and was also expected to be able to learn to talk. At the time, parrots of this sort were described as intelligent, amiable, and charming; as soon as a bird screeched or bit, it was ill-natured or stupid. Through ignorance of the disposition of individual animals, unfortunately, such statements are repeated again and again in new books and technical articles, so that in time one species or another acquires the reputation of an "inferior creature."

Appendices

Scientific Bird Collections

The classification, systematization, and description of all bird species is carried out by natural history institutions almost exclusively. Museums active in the discipline of ornithology generally hold a large assortment of specimens and skins of the most varied bird species in their extensive collections of scientific material. Bird fanciers who pursue their hobby intensively and also wish to obtain a basic knowledge of ornithology should not fail to visit museums of natural history on vacations or other trips.

AUSTRALIA
Melbourne: National Museum of Natural History, Geology, and Ethnology
Perth: Public Library, Museum, and Art Gallery of Western Australia
Sydney: Australian Museum
Sydney: MacLeay Museum of Natural History

AUSTRIA
Vienna: Naturhistorisches Museum

BELGIUM
Antwerp: Natuurwetenschappelijk Museum der Stadt Antwerpen
Brussels: Musée Royal d'Histoire Naturelle de Belgique

CZECHOSLOVAKIA
Prague: National Museum

DENMARK
Copenhagen: Zoological museum of the University of Copenhagen

FRANCE
Lyon: Muséum des Sciences Naturelles
Nancy: Musée d'Histoire Naturelle
Paris: Muséum National d'Histoire Naturelle
Strasbourg: Musée Zoologique de l'Université et de la Ville
Toulouse: Muséum d'Histoire Naturelle et Jardin Zoologique

GERMANY
Augsburg: Naturwissenschaftliches Museum
Berlin: Institut für Spezielle Zoologie und Zoologisches Museum der Humboldt-Universität
Bonn: Zoologischer Forschungs institut und Museum Alexander König
Braunschweig: Staatliches Naturhistorisches Museum
Bremen: Übersee-Museum
Coburg: Naturwissenschaftliches Museum der Coburger Landesstiftung
Darmstadt: Hessisches Landesmuseum
Dresden: Staatliches Museum für Tierkunde
Erlangen: Zoologisches Institut der Friedrich-Alexander-Universität
Frankfurt: Forschungsinstitut und Naturmuseum Senckenberg
Göttingen: Zoologisches Institut der Universität Göttingen
Halle: Zoologisches Institut und Sammlung der Martin-Luther-Universtät
Hamburg: Zoologisches Staatsinstitut und Zoologisches Museum
Hannover: Niedersächsisches Landesmuseum
Kassel: Städtisches Naturkundemuseum
Kiel: Zoologisches Institut und Museum der Universität Kiel
Leipzig: Zoologisches Institut der Karl-Marx-Universität
Leipzig: Naturkundliches MuseumMunich: Zoologische Sammlung des Bayrischen Staates
Stuttgart: Staatliches Museum für Naturkunde
Tübingen: Zoologisches Institut der Universität Tübingen

Wilhelmshafen: Institut für
Vogelforschung

ITALY
Genoa: Museo Civico di Storia
Naturale
Milan: Museo Civico di Storia Naturale
Naples: Museo Zoologico della
Universita
Rome: Museo Civico di Zoologia
Turin: Museo di Zoologia

THE NETHERLANDS
Amsterdam: Zoologisches Museum der
Universiteit Amsterdam
Leyden: Rijksmuseum van Natuurlijke
Historie

NORWAY
Oslo: Zoological Museum of the
University of Oslo

SWEDEN
Göteborg: Natural History Museum
Lund: Zoological Institute and
Museum
Stockhlom: Royal Natural History
Museum

SWITZERLAND
Basel: Museum für Völkerkunde
Genf: Muséum d'Histoire Naturelle
Lausanne: Musée Zoologique de
l'Université Lausanne
Neuchatel: Musée d'Histoire Naturelle

UNITED KINGDOM
Cambridge: University Museum of
Zoology
Edinburgh: Royal Scottish Museum
Tring: British Museum (Natural
History)

UNITED STATES
Cambridge, MA: Museum of
Comparative Zoology
Chicago: Chicago Academy of Sciences
Chicago: Chicago Natural History
Museum
New York: American Museum of

Natural History
San Diego: Natural History Museum
San Francisco: Pacific Museum of
Ornithology
Washington: United States National
Museum (possesses three specimens
of the extinct Culebran form of the
Puerto Rican Amazon, *Amazona
vittata gracilipes*)

The museums listed are only a small
portion of the natural history museums
in the world. Information on visiting
times and opening hours can be
obtained from museum
administrations, or through authorized
tourism officials.

Bird Parks and Zoos
Many national and international
zoological gardens have parrots on
exhibit. The zoos of special interest for
bird fanciers are listed below. No doubt
there are other zoos not mentioned here
that also exhibit rare birds in their
collections.

AUSTRIA
Vienna: Tiergarten Schönbrunn

GERMANY
Berlin: Tierpark Friedrichsfelde
Berlin: Zoologischer Garten Berlin
Cologne: Zoologischer Garten
Lörrach-Baden: Vogelpark Wiesental
Munich: Tierpark Hellabrunn
Stuttgart: Zoologisch-Botanischer
Garten Wilhelma
Walsrode: Vogelpark Walsrode
Wuppertal-Eberfeld: Zoo Wuppertal

THE NETHERLANDS
Amsterdam: Zoologischer Garten
Wasenaar: Tiergerten Wasenaar

SWITZERLAND
Basel: Zoologischer Garten
Zürich: Zoologischer Garten

UNITED KINGDOM
Chester: Chester Zoo
London: London Zoo
Rode (near Bath): The Tropical Bird
    Gardens
Burton-on-the-Water (near Oxford):
    Bird Gardens

UNITED STATES
Chicago: Brookfield Zoo
Houston: Houston Zoo
Miami: Parrot Jungle
San Diego: San Diego Zoo
Tampa: Busch Gardens

Zoos and bird gardens of interest to bird fanciers are found in the larger cities (usually the capitals) in the countries of Central and South America, Africa, Southeast Asia, and Australia. Since many parrots are indigenous to these regions, these animals are often exhibited along with native animal species.

Associations and Specialty Periodicals

In recent years more and more people have found an interest in keeping and breeding birds, so that it is not surprising that associations of bird fanciers have grown steadily. Personal contact with other bird fanciers is facilitated, information can be exchanged, and, additionally, problems of breeding and care can be discussed. Membership in such an association can be recommended to every bird fancier.

The specialty periodicals, which as a rule appear monthly, offer a different way to obtain information. Here one finds detailed reports on feeding problems, accommodations, illnesses, breeding, book reviews, and so on. Following is a list of some of these (and the abbreviations under which they are cited in the Bibliography).

GERMANY
AZ-Nachrichten (AZ), "publication of
    the Central Exchange of German
    bird fanciers and breeders" (G.
    Wittenbrock, Vor der Elm 1, 2860
    Osterholz-Scharmbeck, FRG).
Die Gefiederte Welt (Gef. Welt) (Verlag
    Eugen Ulmer, Wollgrasweg 41, 7000
    Stuttgart 70, FRG).
Die Voliere (Verlag M. & H. Schaper,
    Grazer Str. 20, 3000 Hannover 81,
    FRG).
Geflügel Börse (Verlag Jürgens KG,
    Industriestr. 5, 8035 Gemering 1,
    FRG).
Trochilus (Biotrophic Verlag GmbH,
    Blochmatt 7, 7570 Baden-Baden,
    FRG).
ZZA-Zoologischer Zentral-Anzeiger
    (Zentralverband Zoologischer
    Fachgeschäfte Deutschlands e.V.,
    6057 Dietzenbach 1, Am
    Stadtbrunnen, FRG).

SWITZERLAND
Gefiederter Freund (Gef. Freund) (D.
    Bischofberger, Mühlegasse 31, CH
    6340 Baar/ZG, Switzerland)

UNITED KINGDOM
Avicultural Magazine, journal of the
    Avicultural Society (Windsor Forest
    Stud, Mill Ride, Ascot, Berkshire
    SL5 8LT, England).
Cage and Aviary Birds (Oakfield
    House, Perrymount Road, Haywards
    Heath, Sussex RH16 3DH, UK)
Magazine of the Parrot Society (19a De
    Pary's Avenue, Bedford, England).

UNITED STATES
The A.F.A. Watchbird, journal of the
    American Federation of Aviculture
    (Box 56218, Phoenix, AZ 85079).
American Cage-Bird Magazine (1
    Glamore Court, Smithtown, NY
    11787).
Bird Talk (Box 3940, San Clememte,
    CA 92672).
Bird World (Box 70, North Hollywood,
    CA 91603).
Parrot World, journal of the National
    Parrot Association (8 North
    Hoffman Lane, Hauppauge, NY
    11788).

Bibliography

Austin, O. L., Jr. 1961. *Birds of the world*. New York: Golden Press.

AZ-Nachrichten. *Vogelkrankheiten*. Sonderheft der AZ.

Bedford, 12th Duke of. 1954. *Parrots and parrot-like birds*. Fond du Lac, WI: All-Pets Books [Neptune, NJ: T.F.H. Publications]

Belcher, C., and Smooker, G. D. 1936. Birds of Trinidad and Tobago. *The Ibis* VI: 12–16.

Bernasek, O. 1976. Gelungene Zucht der Kuba-Amazone. *Gef. Welt*, 24–25.

Binford, L. C. 1968. *A preliminary survey of the avifauna of the Mexican state of Oaxaca*. PhD thesis, Louisiana University.

Blake, E. R. 1953. *Birds of Mexico*. Chicago: University of Chicago Press.

Boetticher, H. v. 1962. *Papageien*. Wittenberg-Lutherstadt: A. Ziemsen-Verlag.

Bond, J. 1956. *Check-list of birds of the West Indies*. Philadelphia: Academy of Natural Sciences.

―――. 1971. *Birds of the West Indies*. London: Collins.

Böni, G. 1979. Zucht der Weiszstirn-Amazone. *Gef. Freund*, 157–159.

Dorst, J. 1972. *Die Vögel in ihrem Lebensraum*. Lausanne: Editions Recontre.

Ebert, W. 1978. *Vogelkrankheiten*. Hannover: Schaper.

Eisenmann, E., and Loftin, H. 1968. Birds of the Panama Canal Zone area. *Florida Naturalist* 41: 57–60.

ffrench, R. 1976. *A guide to the birds of Trinidad and Tobago*. Valley Forge, PA: Harrowood Books.

Fink, H. 1979. Zucht der Blaukronen-oder San Domingo-Amazone. *Gef. Freund*, 245–249.

Fisher, J. N. S., and Vincent, J. 1969. *The red book: wildlife in danger*. London: Collins.

Forshaw, J. M. 1973. *Parrots of world*. Melbourne: Lansdowne Press [Neptune, NJ: T.F.H. Publications].

Garrido, O. H., and Schwartz, A. 1968. Anfibio, reptiles y aves de las peninsula de Guanahacabibes, Cuba. *Poeyana*, ser. A. 53: 1–68.

Greenway, J. C., Jr. 1967. *Extinct and vanishing birds of the world*. New York: Dover Publications.

Griscom, L. 1926. The ornithological results of the Mason-Spinden Expedition to Yucatán: Part II, Chinchorro Bank and Cozumel Island. *Amer. Mus. Novit.* 236: 1–13.

Gut, Fr. 1977. Zuchterfolg mit dem Panama Gelbstirn-Amazone. *Gef. Freund*, 164–165.

Harnisch, W. 1975–76. *Mai's Auslandtaschenbuch, Nr. 28: Karibien und Mittelamerika*. Buchenhain: Verlag Volk und Heimat.

Harrison, C. J. O., and Holyoat, D. T. 1970. Apparently undescribed parrot eggs in the collection of the British Natural History Museum. *Bull. Brit. Ornit. Club* 90: 42–46.

Hartert, E. 1893. On the birds of the islands of Aruba, Curaçao, and Bonaire. *Ibis*, 6th ser., 5: 289–338.

Haverschmidt, F. 1968. *Birds of Surinam*. Edinburgh: Oliver and Boyd.

Herklots, G. A. C. 1961. *The birds of Trinidad and Tobago*. London: Collins.

Kepler, C. B. 1970. The Puerto Rican Parrot. In H. T. Odum, *A tropical rain forest*. Oak Ridge, TN: U.S. Atomic Energy Comm. Div. of Technical Information.

Klaas, E. E. 1968. Summer birds from the Yucatán Peninsula, Mexico. *Univ. Kans. Publish. Mus.* 17: 579–611.

Land, H. C. 1970. *Birds of Guatemala.* Wynnewood, PA: Livingston.

Loughlin, E. M. 1970. Field notes on the breeding and diet of some South American parrots. *Foreign Birds* 1970: 169–171.

Low, R. 1972. *The parrots of South America.* London: Gifford.

———. 1980. *Parrots, their care and breeding.* Poole, Dorset: Blandford Press.

Lowery, G. H., Jr., and Dalquest, W. W. 1951. Birds from the state of Veracruz, Mexico. *Univ. Kans. Publis. Mus.* 3: 526–547.

Luther, D. 1970 *Die ausgestorbenen Vögel der Welt.* Wittenberg-Lutherstadt: A. Ziemsen-Verlag.

Mann, B., and Mann, P. 1978. Breeding the Finsch's Amazon. *Magazine of the Parrot Society* 12: 295–297.

Mattmann, J. 1981. Erstzucht von Grünwangen-Amazonen, *Amazona viridigenalis. Gef. Freund*, 2–3.

Meier, A. 1980. Zuchtbericht von der Goldzügel-Amazone. *Gef. Freund*, 189–193.

Meyer de Schauensee, R. 1964. *The birds of Colombia.* Narbeth, PA: Livingston.

———. 1966. *The species of birds of South America.* Wynnewood, PA: Livingston.

———. 1970. *A guide to the birds of South America.* Wynnewood, PA: Livingston.

Mitterhuber, H., and Grahl, W. de. 1979. Seltenheitszucht: Venezuela-Amazone. *AZ*, 46–47.

Moderne Ländlerlexikon, Das. 1979. Gütersloh: Bertelsmann Lexikon-Verlag.

Monroe, B. L., Jr. 1968. *A distributional survey of the birds of Honduras.* New York: AOU Ornithol. Monog. 7: 196.

Müller, H. 1978. Erstzucht von Weiszstirn-Amazonen. *Voliere*, 5–8.

Neunzig, K., and Russ, K. 1921. *Handbuch für Vogelliebhaber, -züchter und -händler.* Magdeburg: Creutzsche Verlagsbuchhandlung.

Nottebohm, F., and Nottebohm, M. 1969. The parrots of Bush Bush. *Animal Kingdom* 72: 19–23.

Olivares, A. 1969. *Aves de Cuncinamarca.* Univ. Nacional de Colombia: Direction de Divulgacion Cultural.

Paynter, R. A., Jr. 1955. The ornithogeography of the Yucatán Peninsula, Mexico. *Peabody Mus. Nat. Hist.* 9: 1–347.

Peters, J. L. 1937. *Check-list of birds of the world.* Cambridge, MA: Harvard University Press.

Peterson, R. T., and Chalif, E. L. 1973. *A field guide to Mexican birds.* Boston: Houghton Mifflin Co.

Phelps, W. H., and Phelps, W. H., Jr. 1958. Lista de las aves de Venezuela con su distribucion: Part 1, Passeriformes. *Boletin de la Sociedad Venezolana de Ciencias Naturales*, vols 19, 90.

Porter, S. 1929. In search of the Imperial Parrot. *Avic. Mag.*, 4th ser., 7: 240–246, 267–275.

Poschung, O. 1978. Freud und Leid einer Zucht der Taubenhals-Amazone. *Gef. Freund*, 245–248.

Prestwich, A. A. 1963. *I name this parrot.* Edenbridge, Kent.

Reichenow, A. 1955. *Vogelbilder aus fernen Zonen—Papageien.* Pfungstadt, Helène.

Rodriguez-Vidal, J. A. 1959. Puerto Rican Parrot study. *Monog. Dep. Agricult. Com., Puerto Rico* I: 1–15.

Russ, K. 1891. *Die Papageien.* Magdeburg: Creutzsche Verlagsbuchhandlung.

Russel, S. M. 1964. A distributional study of the birds of British Honduras. *AOU Monog.* I: 1–95.

Sabel, K. 1961. *Vogelfutterpflanzen.* Pfungstadt: Helène.

Schaldach, W. J., Jr. 1963. The avifauna of Colima and adjacent

Jalisco, Mexico. *Proc. West. Found. Zool.* 1: 1–100.

Schönwetter, M. 1964. *Handbuch der Oologie.* Berlin: Akademie-Verlag.

Sick, H. 1965. A fauna do cerrado. *Arq. Zool. Est. S. Paulo* 12: 71–93.

———. 1968. Vogelwanderungen im kontinentalen Südamerika. *Vogelwarte* 1968: 217–243.

Stager, K. E. 1957. The avifauna of the Tres Marías Islands, Mexico. *Auk* 74: 413-432.

Stone, W., and Roberts, H. R. 1935. Zoological results of the Mato Grosso Expedition in Brazil in 1931, II: Birds. *Proc. Acad. Nat. Sci. Phila.* 86: 363–397.

Vit, R. 1974. Gelungene Blaustirn-Amazonen Zucht. *Gef. Welt,* 61.

Voous, K. H. 1955. *De Vogels von der Nederlandse Antillen.* Curaçao: Natuurwetenschappelijke Werkgroep Nederlandse Antillen.

Voss-Gerling, W. 1969. *Mittlamerika.* Munich: Polyglott-Verlag.

Wetmore, A. 1927. The birds of Porto Rico and the Virgin Islands—Psittaciformes to Passeriformes. *Scient. Suv. Porto Rico,* 409–598.

———. 1968. *The birds of the Republic of Panama.* Washington: Smithsonian Inst. Press.

Wolters, H. E. 1975. *Die Vogelarten der Erde, eine systematische Liste mit Verbreitungsangaben sowie deutschen und englischen Namen.* Hamburg: Paul Parey.

ZZA. 1977-78. *Handbuch des Zoofachhandels.* Zentralverband Zoologischer Fachgeschäfte Deutschlands e.V.

The subspecies of the Red-lored Amazon known as the Lilacine Amazon, *Amazona autumnalis lilacina,* is quite evidently different from the nominate form.

Index

Page numbers in **boldface** refer to illustrations.

189